AS WE SAW THE THIRTIES

AS WE SAW

MAX SHACHTMAN

GERALD L. K. SMITH

GRANVILLE HICKS

NORMAN THOMAS

A. J. MUSTE

HAL DRAPER

BURTON K. WHEELER

EARL BROWDER

THE THIRTIES

Essays on social and political movements of a decade

edited by Rita James Simon

University of Illinois Press
Urbana, Chicago, and London

Second printing, December 1969

 Library of Congress Catalog Card No. 66-15475.

252 74533 7

For David Meyer and Judith Debs

Contents

Introduction

THE 1930'S WAS THE DECADE of hard times. The United States and most of the rest of the world were experiencing the worst economic depression of their history. Archibald MacLeish's poem "Land of the Free," written in 1938, had as its refrain "we don't know, we can't say, we're wondering. . . ." These lines seemed to characterize the spirit of the times.

In 1931, two years after the crash of 1929, twelve million workers were unemployed. That was about 16 per cent of the labor force. In 1933, the percentage rose to 25. In 1938, it was still as high as 19 per cent and as late as 1941, when United States involvement in World War II was only months away, 10 per cent of the labor force was unemployed. Today, in the 1960's, whenever unemployment rises to 5 per cent of the labor force, the President's Council of Economic Advisors officially sounds the alarm. Between 1929 and 1941 the number of people who received federal, state, or local relief has been estimated at between twenty and twenty-five million.

In the spring of 1932, some eight thousand veterans of World War I arrived in Washington, D.C., from all parts of the country to lobby for passage of the Patman Bill. The Patman Bill provided for the immediate payment of a bonus that they were not scheduled to receive until 1945. On June 16, the Senate voted to reject the Patman Bill. A few weeks later after the administration had given wide publicity to its belief that the "march" had been inspired and led by Bolsheviks and other radicals, Congress voted to pay the passage home of the marchers. About five thousand left. The rest were evacuated by the army under the direction of the Chief of Staff, General Douglas MacArthur. In the riot that ensued between marchers and soldiers, two veterans were killed.

The 1930's witnessed the rise of the Congress of Industrial Organizations, and with its rise some of the bitterest and bloodiest strikes of our history. The General Motors strike which opened the way for organizing all of the auto industry lasted forty-four days. It involved 44,000 workers directly, and over one hundred thousand indirectly. Sixty factories in fourteen states did not operate.

The "sit-down" strike attracted national attention during the 1930's. It was used against the Hormel Packing Company in Minnesota in 1933 and by the Goodyear workers in Akron, Ohio, in 1936. The technique was employed again in Michigan against the auto industry and later by shipbuilders, bakers, coal miners and steelworkers. In one year, from 1936 to 1937, almost half a million workers were involved in sit-down strikes. From 1930 to 1937, there were more than 4,700 strikes.

All aspects of life were affected by the depression. Marriage and birth rates dropped drastically. In 1932, the marriage rate per thousand was 7.8 compared to 10.1 in 1929. The birth rate dropped from 18.9 in 1929 to 16.5 in 1933. Many people believed it was immoral to bring children into a world that contained as much ugliness and despair as the world of the 1930's. The divorce rate dropped too: from 1.6 per thousand in 1929 to 1.3 in 1932. Divorce was a luxury few could afford during the depression.

Between 1930 and 1940 the percentage of adolescents who remained in high school rose from 50 to 75. Even at rock-bottom wages, jobs for grown men with experience, skill, and education were hard enough to find; employment opportunities for high school dropouts were almost nonexistent. College students faced blank futures. Recent law graduates were lucky to find jobs as clerks or salesmen. Many department stores in New York City hired only college graduates to run the elevators. *Fortune* magazine in publishing the results of a poll it took of college students in 1937 described them as "fatalistic."

John Steinbeck's novel *The Grapes of Wrath* provided a vivid description of the desperate plight of the Oakies, farmers from Texas, Oklahoma, and Arkansas who lost their land to the dust storms that swept the prairies and who struggled to reach the mecca of the West – California. There they expected to find jobs, land, and hope – instead, they met violence and hostility.

But the 1930's was not only the decade of economic depression. It was also the decade that witnessed the rise of fascism in Europe and Asia. In 1931, Japan invaded Manchuria; in 1937 it attacked China. Mussolini tested his modern war machine against Ethiopia in 1935. In 1937, Italy and Germany helped Franco to destroy the Spanish Republic. Hitler later boasted that he was able to test his new planes, tanks, and other equipment on Spanish battlefields. Before the decade was over, Nazi Germany had marched into the Rhineland, had absorbed parts of Czechoslovakia and all of Austria, and had plunged most of Europe into war.

In the United States, the 1930's will also be remembered as the era of the New Deal and as a period of tremendous social, political, and intellectual ferment. The American people were looking for leaders who had charisma—men who by their own extraordinary powers could change the world from a place of despair to one of hope. Leaders were sought who could provide jobs for husbands and fathers with families to feed and clothe, who could provide opportunity and hope for young people who were getting out of school and had nothing to look forward to, who could offer security to old people who felt ashamed for having lived so long, and who could offer reassurance to those who saw what was happening in Germany and were afraid.

Men arose to answer those needs. Probably in no other single decade in American history were so many plans offered by so many men who believed they could make the sick well, could change feelings of despair into feelings of hope, and could lead the nation out of darkness.

From Louisiana came Senator Huey Long with his program for "Sharing Our Wealth," a scheme that involved the distribution of large fortunes so that every family in the United States could be guaranteed an annual income of at least $2000, and a provision that the government would furnish a homestead allowance free of debt to every family. From Detroit came Father Coughlin with his national Union of Social Justice. Coughlin advocated the nationalization of banks, credit, utilities, and natural resources. He also warned against United States involvement in another "European" war. From California came Dr. Francis Townsend with a plan that would give every citizen sixty years or older a pension of $200 each month. From Harlem came Father Divine with his incantation "Peace, it's wonderful," and a program that provided food and shelter to followers who placed all their savings in his trust. From the labor movement, from farmers, from minority groups, men came forth with answers to the questions they thought the people were asking.

This book records some of the answers provided by some of those leaders. It contains eight transcribed lectures given on the campus of the University of Illinois from October, 1965 through April, 1966 under the auspices of an ad hoc faculty committee. The series was entitled "Leaders of Social and Political Movements in the 1930's." Its basic purpose was to offer to the generation of the sixties the opportunity to hear first person, eyewitness accounts of the purposes and goals of the important movements of the thirties by the men who led those movements — by men whose names are associated with the drama of the depression decade.

Obviously, our list is not exhaustive. Many of these men, such as Huey Long, Father Divine, Francis Townsend, are no longer alive. Some, like John L. Lewis and Margaret Sanger, thought they were too old and too tired to participate. Others, like Father Coughlin and

Robert Hutchins, were too busy. Most of the great figures of the New Deal such as Franklin Delano Roosevelt, Harry Hopkins, Frances Perkins,[1] Harold Ickes, and Henry Wallace, are dead.

Of those who agreed to participate, we asked that they go back thirty or so years to tell us what they were trying to accomplish, that they describe the purposes and goals of their movements, the evils they were most anxious to correct, and the changes they most wanted to make. We asked that they describe their followers and the kinds of people they were trying to reach; that they try to assess how successful they were in accomplishing the goals they set forth, and the importance of the movements they led. What impact did the movement have in its time and what place does it, or will it, occupy in history?

To represent the radical left we invited Norman Thomas, the then and now leader of the American Socialist party; Earl Browder, the head of the American Communist party, who coined the slogan "Communism is 20th Century Americanism"; and Max Shachtman, the leader of a small but extremely vocal Trotskyist group. To represent the Huey Long "Share Our Wealth" program, we invited the Reverend Gerald L. K. Smith, who also led a Christian crusade of his own. To represent labor we invited A. J. Muste, who organized and led some of the most militant strikes in our history. From the world of writers and artists we called upon Granville Hicks, who in the thirties was literary editor of *New Masses*. To represent the student movement we invited Hal Draper, who led a national peace strike from Brook-

[1] Mrs. Perkins had agreed to participate but she died a few months before her scheduled talk.

lyn College in 1935. Finally, to talk about his experiences with the New Deal and about his leadership of the American Isolationist Movement, we invited the former senator from Montana, Burton K. Wheeler.

Funds for the series came from the University of Illinois Foundation and were released to us by Provost Lyle Lanier. The College of Journalism and Communications, the Institute of Labor and Industrial Relations, and the Sociology Department also helped finance the series. A special debt of gratitude is owed to the staff of the Institute of Communications Research for keeping the records and managing the books.

As chairman of the ad hoc faculty committee, I want to acknowledge the help and support I received from my colleagues, Professors Murray Edelman, James W. Carey, Howard S. Maclay, and Joseph R. Gusfield.

I owe two personal debts of gratitude, one to my husband for his advice during the planning and arranging stages and for his help after the speakers had arrived on campus. The second debt is owed to my daughter, Judith Debs, for the consideration she showed in the timing of her arrival. She was born after Granville Hicks and before A. J. Muste.

MAX SHACHTMAN

Radicalism in the Thirties: The Trotskyist View

Introduction by Howard Maclay

Max Shachtman has traveled more political miles than any of the other participants in the series. He began his long career in radical politics at sixteen when he was one of the founders of the American Communist party in 1920. Eight years later, he and two other members of the Central Committee, Cannon and Abern, were expelled from the party for "Trotskyism." Shachtman then became one of the founders of the American International Trotskyist Movement and the editor of its press.

Although the Trotskyists were the most radical of all the left-wing groups in the thirties and attracted a good deal of comment and attention, it is unlikely that their membership ever exceeded a thousand people. Of all the groups aligned

Howard Maclay is the director of the Institute of Communications Research, University of Illinois.

on the political continuum to the left of the Democratic party, the Communists and the Trotskyists were the most bitter toward each other. It was the Trotskyists who were the first to publicize the "truth" about the Stalinist regime, and during the period of the Moscow Show Trials in the mid-thirties it was the Trotskyists who sought to arouse a basically indifferent American public to the meaning of those trials.

Max Shachtman was born in Warsaw in 1904. When he was slightly under a year old his parents arrived with him in New York City, where he has lived most of his life. He attended the public schools in New York and for a brief period was a student at the City College of New York.

In 1940, during the period of the Hitler-Stalin Pact, Shachtman and Leon Trotsky had a parting of the political ways. Trotsky advocated unconditional support of the Soviet Union and Shachtman advocated neutrality. After Trotsky's death in August of 1940, Shachtman was named administrator of Trotsky's literary estate. In that capacity he has edited and translated into English many of Trotsky's works.

At the present time, Max Shachtman is a member of the American Socialist party.

THE 1930's MADE UP A DECADE unique in the history of American radicalism. It was so distinctive that, taken on the whole, its like was never known in the generations that preceded it, or in the generations that followed. Of all the elements that determined the character and development of radicalism in the thirties, three were outstanding. One was the economic and political crisis precipitated by the stock market crash in 1929—the crisis that was thereafter delicately referred to as the Depression, as if to soften its intensity, its depth, and its impact. The second was the beginning of that stupendous transformation of Russian society that gave substance and shape to the phenomenon of Stalinism. And the third was the consolidation of power of Hitlerite fascism in central Europe.

The two main branches of American radicalism in the 1930's, as in the 1920's, were the communist and socialist movements — the Communist and Socialist parties — with the newly arisen Trotskyist movement forming a significant, but minor division. The way in which each of them reacted to the three outstanding and profoundly interrelated elements of the time, the way in which each understood the problems they posed, and the solutions each saw for the problems — these constitute the turbulent chronicle of American radicalism in the thirties.

As the twenties were coming to an end, American radicalism seemed to be obsolete. Years of relative prosperity under Harding and Coolidge and for a short time under Hoover had successfully isolated and paralyzed a declining radical world. The Socialist party was still bleeding heavily from the wounds inflicted by successive Communist splits. And the Communist party was bleeding from self-inflicted wounds of incessant internal, factional conflicts which were almost incomprehensible to outside observers and hardly more comprehensible to inside participants.

The once spectacular IWW had all but died out completely. The Farmer Labor party movement of the early twenties collapsed after the defeat of Senator La Follette in the 1924 presidential election. The official labor movement of that time was conservative, narrow, smug, and small. Before it was split in 1919, the united Socialist party had well over a hundred thousand dues-paying members in its ranks. It is certain that the Communist and Socialist parties had less than 20,000 members between them ten years later when the crisis erupted. But the crisis did erupt, and as American capitalism was sinking to its depression, American radicalism began rising out of its own.

The Communist party did not immediately benefit to any substantial degree from the consequences of the crisis, certainly not to the extent of converting itself into the real political force that it became later on. The reason for this delay lies primarily in the fact that for it the decade was divided into two almost equal halves. During the first half, it thought and acted under the dogma of what the Communist International, from the years 1928 onward, called the "Third Period." The theory and practice of the "Third Period" were a manifestation of political insanity never before known in the radical movement and, happily, never repeated since.

According to the new Communist doctrine, events since the First World War ended were divided into three periods. The first was the period of unprepared and unsuccessful storm assault upon European capitalism, which proved stout enough to defeat it. The second period was that of the relative stabilization of capitalism. And the "Third Period," which was now ushered in, was the period of the final collapse of capitalism throughout the world and its burial under the revolutionary offensive of the proletariat led by the Communist parties.

As an analysis, this was more than risky. Perfectly disastrous, however, were the consequences of its corollary. This was the theory of "Social Fascism." How shall I explain this theory to you, more than thirty years later? This theory was fathered by Stalin himself, which in those days meant a good deal. According to him, fascism and social democracy—the socialist movement—were not adversaries, they were twins. According to this utterly incredible doctrine, in the "Third Period" of the decay of capitalism and the rise of fascist movements, the socialist parties had been transformed from the right wing of the labor movement into the moderate wing of fascism. It has become "Social Fascism"— socialist in words, but fascist in reality.

It is hard to believe, a generation later, what the Communists drew from this revelation and what they added to it. Throughout the world, from Warsaw to Berlin to Paris to London to New York to Shanghai, the doctrine proclaimed the policy that the main enemy of the working class in its fight against capitalism and fascism, and for socialist power was the "Socialist Fascists." They had to be crushed first of all, before fascism, let alone capitalism itself, could be smashed. Monstrous though this was, a whole series of similar weirdnesses were added to it. Everything and everybody outside the Communist party was designated as a variety of fascism. That Hoover was a fascist went without saying; and so was the American Congress under his administration. Roosevelt, during his first years in office, was not one whit better—if anything, worse—because he only masqueraded as a liberal. Left-wing socialists, especially those with a friendly attitude toward the Communists, could not deceive them for a minute: they were *left* "Social Fascists," who tried to hide their aid to fascism under the cunning pretense of being radical. Anarchists and syndicalists who had always been known as anarchists and syndicalists—a not illogical way of designating them—were designated henceforth as nothing but "Anarcho-

Fascists" and "Syndicalo-Fascists." As for Trotskyists, it leaped to the eye that they were nothing but "Trotskyo-Fascists." The closer any of these groupings were, or seemed to be, to the Communist party, the more dangerous they were to it, and the more ruthlessly they had to be opposed, denounced, and destroyed.

The type of ultra-radicalism which demands, or at least guarantees in advance, the increase to the maximum of your opponents and the reduction to a minimum of your friends, had been known before then and since then, down to the very days in which we are now living. But the theory and practice of "Social Fascism" was in a class by itself — a special case history in organized, systematically inflicted political dementia injected for tragical years into the veins of every Communist party in the world, like some hallucinatory drug which evokes fantasies of power in the mind without adding one real ounce of strength to the body. In Germany in 1933 — and in the rest of the world as a sequel to the fascist victory — the consequences of this theory were calamitously sinister.

As a result, the gains of the American Communists during the first half of the thirties were decidedly modest, especially in the light of radical moods which were growing out of the social discreditment of a capitalism incapable of solving the depression. The Communist party made no real headway in the official labor movement, for the organized and still-employed workers were fearful to strike, or even to demand very much when the factory gates were crowded every day with the unemployed, desperately eager to take their places. The party did make some headway among the unemployed and did succeed in organizing large demonstrations throughout the country, and in repeating them every day and every week. But unemployed workers are not a very sturdy or durable basis for a political movement, as all those engaged in work among them soon discovered.

Among radical intellectuals, including many who had never been radicals before, the Communist party made more progress. In support of its candidate for the presidency of the United States in 1932, the party mustered the support of a large roster of some of the most prominent and influential intellectuals, writers, poets, and artists in the country. Indeed, for a time it seemed that the Communist party would gain and maintain a monopoly in the realm of the intellectuals, so explosive was the reaction for the apparent final collapse of the capitalist economy among warm-thinking, socially minded men and women of ideas and of art. But even of these intellectual supporters it can be said that most of them were not attracted so much by the grotesqueness of the theory of "Social Fascism" as they were by the apparent growth and militancy of German communism in its opposition to fascism, by the self-sacrificing devotion and the tireless readiness for aggressive action, and by the intransigent anticapitalism of the Communists in this country at that time.

The early thirties also showed some revival of the Socialist party. In fact for a time it seemed that it might outstrip the Communists, for the first time in almost a decade, as the dominant party in American radicalism. Its ranks too were pushed to the left by the crisis in the country. New and young trade unionists, vigorous, combative, idealistic, came into its ranks in very considerable numbers. So did thousands of young people, children of workers and of ruined middle-class elements who had no visible prospects of employment in industry, or of a career in the professional or academic world. So also did many formerly nonsocialist reformers and liberals, repelled by the policies of the Communists but attracted to the Socialist party mainly because of its militant activity in behalf of countless worthy causes, its great social idealism, and the integrity of the man who was becoming the party's chief spokesman – Norman Thomas. The new growth in the Socialist party, and its shift to the left, was sustained even after the left wing in it won the party leadership and adopted an exceedingly radical program in 1934, despite the abandonment of the party by its old moderate leadership, the so-called Old Guard. But it was not sustained for long. The reasons for the ensuing setback of the Socialist party were soon to become evident.

The thirties also saw a movement new to American radicalism, the Trotskyists. They deserve attention, not because they ever became or really could have become a major political force, and not even because they were a numerical force, but because the influence of their ideas expanded far beyond anything they ever achieved in membership.

In actual point of time, the Trotskyist movement was established in 1928. Up to then Trotsky, who had had considerable support in many of the European Communist parties, had found none in the American party, except for the vague and doubtful sympathy of one party leader, who was himself expelled in 1925 without ever having become a Trotskyist. Outside the Communist party, Trotsky had the support of the then-prominent communist intellectual, Max Eastman, who was the first person to make public the famous "Testament" of Lenin and later the Trotskyist platform in Russia, neither of which had any effect upon the American communist movement at that time.

It was only after the leader of one of the smallest factions in the Communist party, James P. Cannon, returned from the Sixth World Congress of the Communist International in 1928 did Trotskyism obtain a foothold in this country. Cannon was persuaded of the correctness of Trotsky's position after reading his polemical criticism of the official Communist International program which was circulated among very few of the Congress delegates in badly bowdlerized form, in a bad translation, and with the strict injunction that it be returned after reading. Cannon literally had to steal a copy and smuggle it out of Russia to bring it into the United States.

By 1928, Trotskyism was already so abhorrent a heresy in the Communist parties that Cannon could show his copy of Trotsky's critique secretly only to two or three of his most intimate friends. And these agreed with him to start a highly discreet effort to win the support of other party members. The atmosphere of that time may be judged from the fact that old and trusted party leaders, such as these were, had to organize themselves with conspiratorial prudence to make possible nothing more than a discussion of Trotsky's views. But prudence and discretion did not avail them much time. The secret leaked out in less time than it takes to say Cannon, Abern, and Shachtman. These men were called before the party Central Committee, of which they were members, and after a few hours of probing and fencing, the trio flatly announced that they were indeed in agreement with the Russian Trotskyist opposition. Thereupon, and without one moment's delay, they were all summarily expelled from the Central Committee and from the party which they had helped to found. There was no trial of any kind, no discussion at all of the validity of Trotsky's views. Merely to share his views was grounds for automatic, instantaneous expulsion.

The three Trotskyists might have been a long time growing beyond that number if they had not immediately been given unsolicited aid from the leadership that ousted them. When the official announcement of the expulsion was made in the party many members were bewildered, if not stunned, by the news. Some members, instead of voting an endorsement of the expulsion on the ultimative demand of the Central Committee, voted to ask for a discussion of the matter, or for hearing the side of the expelled, or for some simulacrum of a fair consideration of the dispute – three absolutely absurd points of view. The answer they received was an expulsion from the party. In this way the expelled obtained their first reinforcement of two or three score supporters who joined their modest ranks. But further progress was neither easy nor swift.

It is difficult to convey the extraordinary hostility of the party leadership to the tiny Trotskyist group, a hostility with which they soon imbued most of the ranks. For crudeness and intensity, it was without parallel even in the Communist world. The source of this hostility was deep and it was strong: the overwhelmingly passionate attachment that every Communist had to the Soviet regime, to its leadership as the incarnation of the Bolshevik Revolution, of the first socialist state, of the state which was under constant siege from a hated encircling capitalist world. Moreover, consciously or half-consciously, practically every Communist felt that any weakening (let alone any undermining of this state, embodied in its leadership) meant a corresponding weakening and ultimate destruction of the communist movement itself. Whereas, no matter how many defeats it might suffer, the preservation of the Russian state and its leadership was the main guarantee of the growth and final triumph of the Communist party everywhere. A communist movement without Communist Russia, was inconceivable. This concept, however defective, was entirely understandable. It was bred into the bone of every serious Communist and became the distinguishing mark of his political outlook, of his party loyalty, of his psychology and personal behavior.

Trotsky and his supporters could claim, as they did repeatedly, their loyalty to the Bolshevik Revolution, to its principles and ideals, including the principles that lay at the foundation of the Communist International. Their sincerity in this was wholly above question. But they added that this loyalty did not preclude, but on the contrary demanded, the right to criticize policies and leaders that diverged from these principles and these ideals, that brought injury upon them, that denied the right of friendly but free and democratic discussion.

By 1928 virtually all Communist ears were deaf to such views. The official view had become the common view in the ranks of the movement, namely, that Trotskyism was counter-revolutionary, and that its views and criticisms aimed at the overthrow of the socialist state and the restoration of capitalism. And what can antagonize, indeed infuriate, Communist ranks or most of them, more surely than a criticism of the Russian regime not in the language of capitalists or social democrats, but in the language of Communism itself, the language which was the natural tongue of Trotskyism?

In the years to follow, the Trotskyists were to learn that the Communists' attitude toward them became worse, not better—sharper and more embittered, not more conciliatory. To this rule there were a few exceptions in the ranks; but they were decidedly exceptions, and they were never tolerated in the official party.

It was not necessary to wait for the years to follow. When the expelled try to sell the first issue of their fortnightly paper—a radical group without a paper is a contradiction in terms—they were set upon by a mob of their good comrades of yesterday, who ripped the papers out of their hands, and threatened to beat them to the ground, presumably in order to preserve the Soviet Union. Any doubts of the reality of these threats were speedily dispelled for us. The first public meeting called by the tiny handful of Trotskyists was filled by radicals of all kinds interested in hearing the new position to which attention had already been called by fierce, daily denunciations of the expelled by the Communist press. Before the chairman could start the meeting, the doors were forced open by a crowd of a hundred party officials and members, armed with lead pipes, blackjacks, clubs, knives, and similar persuasive arguments, and they succeeded in breaking up the meeting by violent rioting.

The speakers on the platform—who were not allowed to speak—could not believe what they saw being done by men whom they had known by name and record, with whom they had worked as comrades for years. It was only thanks to a sturdy guard of honor, made up of sympathizers and friends and others who insisted on the right of free speech, that the Trotskyists were able, two weeks later in the same hall, to make their first public speeches, and even then only after bloody fights throughout the hall, which was again invaded by armed Communist disrupters. It took three to four years before the Trotskyists were able to hold their meetings in peace, free from threats of organized Communist party violence.

In earlier days, I had to suffer, as did many other Communist speakers and organizers, from the violent disruptions of Communist party and Young Communist League meetings in southern Illinois coal fields—by armed bands of Ku Klux Klan hoodlums who threatened us in limb and life. In the early thirties there was hardly a Trotskyist meeting that I spoke at from coast to coast, and the same held true for other speakers, that did not suffer from the same threats of violence at Communist hands. In Salt Lake City, Utah, a tough Irishman, the local attorney of the American Civil Liberties Union who chaired my meeting only because of his devotion to free speech, had to draw an old western Colt .45 at the podium to warn a threatening Communist mob in the hall that they could not make an assault on the platform with impunity. In Los Angeles, an armed Communist mob succeeded in breaking up my meeting after a dozen people on both sides of the fight lay beaten and bloody on the floor of the hall. It is true that the Klansmen acted in the name of a chauvinist patriotism, of white supremacy, of preserving American womanhood from Negroes, Catholics, and Jews, while the Communist acted in the name of the working class and of socialism. There was that difference. To the

Trotskyists in those days, the difference was not consoling.

It should be noted that the Communists in those days did not conceal their violent attacks on the Trotskyists. One of the leaders of the party wrote openly in the official press in these words, "Why do we break up Trotskyist meetings? Because they are demonstrations against the Soviet Union of the same type as monarchist and socialist demonstrations." I do not know of any monarchist meetings ever held in this country. And if any were held, I never heard of one being broken up by the Communists. Perhaps they felt that they did not then have enough forces to go around. Since they could not stop fascists from speaking, the next best thing to do was to stop "Social Fascists," who after all were the greater danger. For it was not only Trotskyist meetings that were disrupted by organized gangs. The Communists took their "Third Period" and "Social Fascism" seriously. More than one socialist meeting was attacked. Most notable was the huge meeting organized for the Socialist party in 1934 at Madison Square Garden in New York City to pay tribute to the socialist workers who had fought and fallen so bravely in Vienna to defend themselves from the rifles and artillery of Austrian fascism. Literally hundreds of Communists, led by a prominent spokesman of the party and armed with their now-customary arguments invaded the vast hall and broke up the meeting in an orgy of violence that ended with countless injuries and perhaps worse, a scandal and disgrace and bitterness that took years to forget.

It was in connection with this meeting that the first open break occurred between the Communist party and the intellectuals who had supported it. Such men of repute in those days as Edmund Wilson, John Dos Passos, John Chamberlain, Meyer Schapiro, and numerous others addressed an open letter to the Communist party which denounced "the culpability and shame of the Communists" in their assault on the Madison Square Garden meeting. Two years later every one of these men and many more of their kind had broken completely with the Communist party.

These attacks did not discourage the Trotskyists, nor did they halt their progress. On the contrary, they soon won them a good deal of sympathy in part because they were victims of hoodlumism, in part because of their courage and steadfastness. Yet the organization grew very slowly. Material resources were exceedingly scanty, and after six years of existence it was still short of 500 members throughout the country. Not every member had a job, unemployment in the country was still running ten to twelve million or more, and those who were working had modest incomes and little to spare. Many, perhaps most, of its members were young people, sons and daughters of working-class families, part and parcel of what was so truly called the locked-out generation. Well-to-do sponsors and contributors were regrettably unknown. All the more remarkable were its achievements, above all in the field of publications. It succeeded in getting out a weekly newspaper, even though every once in a while poverty dictated the skipping of an issue; and a presentable monthly theoretical revue. Its small but compact youth organization managed with some irregularity to put out a monthly paper of its own. In addition it published at certain periods of time little newspapers in the Yiddish language, in Greek, and even a few issues in the Polish language. Most important to it, however, were the writings of Trotsky, which it translated and published—a whole series of them in pamphlet form and another series in book form. All of this took Herculean efforts. Interested outsiders simply could not believe that all this was being done by only a few hundred people. They assumed that the Trotskyists numbered in the thousands. That it was done year in and year out is an indication of the extent of the dedication, the capacity for work and personal sacrifice, and the confidence of its membership.

The overriding concern of the Trotskyists was a complex of questions of communist theory, principle, and tactics, and these can be very complex. It would be a mistake to suppose that they confined themselves to a study of sacred texts and abstruse polemics. That they did in ample amounts. Yet every member, young or old, was constantly urged—it would not be wrong to say he was required—to join and be consistently active in wider organizations.

Workers who were not already in trade unions were called upon to join one for which they were eligible. Unemployed, including those who were too young to have ever held a job, were prodded, wherever that proved necessary, to find a job, and to join the labor movement, for the Trotskyists always felt a deep commitment to the trade union movement, to its struggles and to its political advancement.

Unemployed who could find no jobs at all were all in one or another of the many councils or other organizations of the out-of-work. Others, who had to subsist on relief, were active in organizations of relief recipients that then existed. Or they belonged to one or another of the tenants' organizations, active among other things in challenging the authorities who evicted tenants from their homes for nonpayment of rent by moving back the pitiful sticks of furniture that were put out on the streets by the marshalls.

Students were active night and day in various radical and left-wing student organizations that experienced a considerable growth in the thirties. And the Trotskyist youth, who was generally far better schooled and skilled in matters of Marxist theory, history, and tactics than the student of any other group, was a factor to be contended with by the other political faiths. In the unending debates, he rarely took as much as he gave.

A good deal of the modest recruitment attained by the Trotskyist movement came from workers active in the trade unions, many of them with a background of experience in the radical political movements – communist or socialist – but they did not bulk too large in the organization. The larger and more continuous flow into its ranks was made up of young people, some of whom the Trotskyists won over from the youth groups of the Communist or Socialist parties, but most of whom they recruited afresh, without previous radical affiliation. These were soon integrated into the organization by the older group, a cadre of experienced Communists with years of political and organizational training behind them, and with the acquired habit of working together despite internal strain and the conflicts which were seldom lacking. The Trotskyists, young and old, were students of serious problems, and even those problems that might seem remote or irrelevant to others were never treated lightly or scoffingly by them.

The cement that held them together was the conviction that the Trotskyist movement sooner or later would displace the official Communist movement as the revolutionary party of the working-class vanguard, cast in the mold of the authentic Leninist party that won the Bolshevik Revolution in 1917.

It goes without saying that Rooseveltism and the New Deal had not the slightest attraction to the Trotskyists. That was capitalist reformism and as such it could never seriously solve the grave social problems that confronted American society in the 1930's. A concrete and practical political alternative to the New Deal, to its shortcomings and defects, was never really considered to be within the purview of the Trotskyist movement. The New Deal was analyzed theoretically, even if not always in its most appropriate significance. It was criticized politically but without the presentation of any political program to counter it that might have appeal to those who were not already committed to a fundamental socialist position.

The main task of the Trotskyist movement, as it saw it and propounded it, was to reconstitute the authentic Communist party and Communist International. The precondition for this was the exposure of the official communist movement for having abandoned the basic principles of communism both in Russia and the capitalist world. That movement was regarded as increasingly reformist and nationalist. The "Third Period" policy was only a temporary zig-zag to the left which would inevitably be followed by a deeper and longer move to the right. That was in accordance with the inner nature of Stalinism. And its inner nature was driving it to the transformation of the once-communist movement into a classical social-democratic movement.

Since in Trotskyist theory this transformation had its

roots in Stalin's subversion of the revolutionary workers' state to the point where capitalism would gradually or catastrophically be restored in Russia—each of the factions in the Russian conflict accused the other of working for the restoration of capitalism and each in his own way was entirely wrong—the center of gravity, so to speak, of the Trotskyist movement was necessarily located in Russia. Its fate could not escape the bonds that tied it to the evolution of the Russian state.

Now this in itself might not have been of fatal consequences to the Trotskyist movement in the achievement of its goal, that of replacing the Communist parties with what it regarded itself to be, the nucleus for the true Communist party. In other words, if its analysis of the meaning and evolution of Stalinism had been correct, its prospects might well have been bright, certainly far brighter than they ever were in reality. If Stalinism meant increasing concessions in Russia to the rich peasants, to the budding capitalist elements of a town, to the purely nationalist development implied in Stalin's theory of "socialism in one country"; if it meant, as Trotsky's indictment read, that Stalinism was the channel through which capitalist restorationist elements were flowing back into power to Russia; if it meant, as Trotsky's indictment read further, that the Communist parties abroad were forced by Moscow to give up revolutionary class struggle and internationalism in favor of class cooperation and nationalism; then the vacuum left behind by this renunciation would of necessity be filled with a new revolutionary communist or Trotskyist movement.

This analysis seemed strictly logical and it held together the Trotskyist movement like a magnet. The difficulty lay in this: In its fundamental aspects, in its fundamental forecasts, the analysis was wrong. Much that Trotsky wrote against the Stalinist regime was deeply and brilliantly true and telling; and much that he predicted about the Stalinist course was remarkably verified by later events. But the central, axial thesis about Stalinism that Trotsky insistently defended was not verified at all. Capitalism was not restored under Stalin, but was wiped out down to the last meaningful vestige. And if Stalin did not establish socialism—as I believe he did not—he decidedly did not re-establish or facilitate the re-establishment of capitalism that Trotsky had forecast. Nor did the evolution of the Communist parties abroad follow the path Trotsky was sure it would follow. Therewith, basically, was eliminated all possibility of the Trotskyist movement attaining its professed role, the role that it was unshakeably convinced for a long time that it was destined to play. But if it did not attain this role—because as is my belief it could not—it does not follow that it played no role at all. It did play a role. It was an important role, and it was played in the very thirties that are now under review.

Quite unlike the first half of the thirties, American radicalism in the second half was not only dominated but was overwhelmingly dominated by the communist movement. The second half can be said to date, with calendar accuracy, from 1935 onward. Just before that period opened, the Trotskyist movement seemed to be gaining real wind in its sail. In 1934 it registered its outstanding success—given its size, it might even be said to be its most spectacular success—in the labor movement. That lay in its ability to organize and build a powerful local of the Teamsters' Union in Minneapolis and to lead it in a bitterly fought, but adeptly conducted strike that shook the whole city of Minneapolis and even the whole state of Minnesota. In Minneapolis, the Trotskyist organization was built around an exceptionally capable group of experienced trade unionists whom it had inherited from the Communist party expulsions in 1928. It was known far and wide that the Teamsters' leaders were Trotskyists, but that did not adversely affect the leaders of the union or the effectiveness of the strike, which was supported not only by the entire local labor movement, but even by the farmers throughout the state.

Governor Olson declared martial law in the city and Cannon and I, who had gone to Minneapolis to cooperate with our comrades and to help them in the publication of their unique daily strike newspaper, were deported under armed National Guard escort from Minneapolis to St. Paul—from which we returned to Minneapolis a few hours later in a discreet automobile. (At such times there is nothing like a discreet automobile.) The reputation of the Trotskyists and the respect for them as people who knew not only all about theory, but who could also conduct an effective strike with practical competence and all sorts of sparkling innovations, was enormously enhanced in radical circles throughout the country. That's how impressive the Minneapolis strike was.

The achievement brought new recruits to the Trotskyists, especially in Minnesota itself, but the organizational gains were far inferior to the gain in reputation. To the outside admirer, as well as to the new recruit, it soon became apparent that Minneapolis was an isolated, essentially local phenomenon due to exceptional and even accidental circumstances, and that the Trotskyist movement was not at all in a position to repeat its sensational performance anywhere else in the country.

Minneapolis, however, did have another positive result for the Trotskyists. In 1933 and 1934, a new radical formation took shape under the name of the American Workers party and under the leadership of A. J. Muste. Its appearance followed the utterly disastrous failure of the Communist and Socialist parties of Germany to prevent Hitlerism from taking power, or even to offer effective resistance to the Nazis. The Musteites, as they were known, wanted a new, truly American radical party, independent of both the socialists and the communists. Only a handful of them had been previously affiliated with a radical political organization. It was a grass roots movement. And if it was a pretty small one, its members were spirited and had acquired experience and the reputation of good and honorable militants in the struggles of the textile, mining, and automobile workers, as well as in a considerable movement of the unemployed that it organized and led.

The Musteites did not at first want to have anything to do with the Trotskyists, whom they regarded as Russian — not American — oriented. They saw the Trotskyists as sectarians, as internal faction fighters, as hair-splitting Talmudists, and as abstract theoreticians. But the outstanding success in Minneapolis began to blunt the edge of this antagonism and to drain it of color. The Trotskyists took the initiative in proposing a fusion with the new American Workers party, and the formation of a united party, on the basis of a protective parity for both sides. The initial opposition to this merger began to weaken and gradually to wither away. Among others, the two leading intellectuals of the American Workers party, Dr. Sidney Hook and James Burnham, urged with increasing vigor and success the acceptance of the Trotskyist proposal. After a few months of negotiation, the union was consummated at an enthusiastic joint convention that founded the Workers Party of the United States.

For American Trotskyism this was indeed a triumph — an infusion of fresh and lusty blood from an unexpected source. It seemed as though the preceding years of study, of discussion, and of theoretical and political preparation were now paying dividends, and that the great goal of a new revolutionary political party (it was the first time the Trotskyists had given themselves the name of party) had been brought a good and firm leap closer.

It was highly encouraging. A great excitement and promise of early and rapid advance prevailed in the new party. Alas, it was mostly illusion. The united party did not quite reach the figure of one thousand members to begin with, and it did not reach beyond this during its brief and rocky career. Almost everything was against it from the beginning.

To start with, a couple of its most prominent figures withdrew from the unity to join the Communist party, including Louis Francis Budenz who was to return to the Catholic Church of his youth, and who became a specialist at exposing the "Red Menace" of the Communist party later on. Then a number of other original Musteites dropped out of the new party and out of all political activity. They could not adapt themselves to the life in which, generally speaking, the Trotskyists felt at home: preoccupation with theoretical questions; refined precision in the formulating of political positions;

a deep interest in all, even the most remote, questions of revolutionary policy in other countries of the world, a passionate opposition to the Stalinist regime in Russia and to the Communist party in the United States, and the like.

To make matters worse, an ultra-radical section of the Trotskyists looked upon the Musteites as politically naive and primitive, at best, and "Centrists" at worst. They launched a campaign to "Bolshevize" the Musteites as quickly as possible. This did not generate much enthusiasm among the Musteites, who did not relish being "Bolshevized" quickly, or slowly, or at all. Finally, most of the Musteites grew worried with fear that the Trotskyists were planning to scuttle the new party and to take it into the Socialist party—a tactic which Trotsky himself had developed at the time for most of the European Trotskyist organizations.

What followed was a veritable shambles of factional strife that paralyzed all activity and foreclosed all possibility of significant growth. The Musteites, dismayed by the spectacle that they ascribed to the incurable Trotskyist maladies of sectarianism, hair-splitting, and schism, dropped away one after another. Not long thereafter Muste himself, returning from a visit to Trotsky in Norway, saw, as he later wrote, a vision of the Christ in the Cathedral of Notre Dame in Paris, and abandoned Trotskyism and Marxism altogether, to become a Gandhian pacifist. The Trotskyists, who by now had indeed decided in favor of joining the Socialist party, although it was not their original position, began to undergo a series of splits in their own ranks which plagued them for years to come, and which it is painful to recall.

One group after another split away from the Trotskyist movement, only to split again, and then once more. Like the amoeba, they multiplied by dividing. One thought the Trotskyist movement was going too far to the right, and had to be fought by a genuinely original-type Trotskyist movement, even if without and against Trotsky. Another denounced the decision to join the Socialist party as a monstrosity, and split away. Another split because the Trotskyists did not regard the Russian regime as capitalist. Still another split away because Russia was not analyzed as a feudal state. Yet another because the Trotskyists supported the Spanish Loyalists in the Civil War, instead of fighting against both the Loyalists and the fascists. And besides them, there were, alas, others. Each constituted a new organization whose program was as clear of deviations as its ranks were of members. Each of these groupings had an elaborate program, an elaborate name — and of course a periodical filled with inconceivable resolutions and theses which scorned the dimensions of breadth and depth and concentrated exclusively on length. All of them announced their readiness to lead the American workers in the struggle to achieve a socialist America through the formation of a truly authentic revolutionary party, free of all deviations, but amply supplied with programs and resolutions for all imaginable problems, and for some that were unimaginable. It was a depressing spectacle. Naturally none of these monastic groupings had the breath of life in them. All of them marched resolutely into early oblivion, together with their programs, their polemics and their periodicals, which thereafter became the rarest of collector's items for specialized students of political anthropology.

Infinitely more important was the complete turnabout-face begun in 1935 by the Communist party here and throughout the world. The entire political and theoretical baggage of the "Third Period" was discarded as if it had never existed, and the era of the "Popular Front" was trumpeted in. The change was breathtaking. So were the consequences.

The call for a Soviet America under a dictatorship of the Communist party which openly proclaimed that it would suppress all other political parties – Republican, Democratic, Socialist, and of course, the Trotskyist – was completely silenced. The party announced that socialism was not at all the goal, or even the issue in American politics; indeed, that the demand for socialism stood in the way of real progress. So moderate a project as the formation of a farmer labor party was soon rejected, and the Communist party became at first a tacit and then an open supporter of the Democratic party and the New Deal as the arena for a new political alignment for the country.

It announced that communism was nothing less and nothing more than twentieth-century Americanism. George Washington, Thomas Jefferson, and Abraham Lincoln were added to the idols of Marx and Lenin and soon superseded them in order of importance. The authenticated American colonial ancestry of the party leader became an increasingly emphasized point of pride, and so was his musical Kansas twang. Aid and comfort, defense and expansion of democracy, a unity of practically everybody in the country against fascism, reaction and war – this was now put forward as the alpha and omega of all Communist politics. The appalling vituperation of everybody outside the Communist party was henceforth reserved only for the extreme right wing of the Republican party, and at the other end of the political spectrum, for the Trotskyists and the more radical Socialists.

Everything that had distinguished Communists from Socialists at the time of the historic split between them after the First World War was sunk without a trace. In fact, the "Popular Front" position of the Communist party on all questions of theory and politics would have repelled the most extreme right-wing socialist at the time of the split in 1919.

With regard to its blind, unquestioning, and uncritical fealty to the Moscow regime, the party became more intolerantly rabid, if that were possible, than it was before. Accordingly, its hostility toward the Trotskyists was only intensified. With the full unfolding of its "Popular Front" course, the unprecedented advance of American communism was assured. Left-wing Socialist and Trotskyist critics were helpless to stem it.

The convergence of political factors in that period was exceptionally favorable to the Communists. Never before or since was the party presented with such extraordinary good fortune. It is only necessary to list the factors which reinforced each other to the Communists' advantage. First there was the New Deal, which, despite its numerous ameliorative measures that enabled capitalism to rise to its feet and limp along, instead of crawling helplessly on its knees, nevertheless, did not succeed in wiping out massive unemployment and industrial distress. In contrast came the sensational reports of the industrial and agricultural revolutions in Russia under Stalin, while only wisps of smoke, or not smoke at all, came out of American plant chimneys. Agricultural problems were being solved by the order to plow under crops and destroy pigs while millions suffered deprivation. Multiplying reports from Russia showed new plants and whole new industries being built, hydroelectric dams being constructed, vast canal systems being dug, new roads being laid, and giant farms being established to augment the production of food and fiber. The noted literary critic, Edmund Wilson, once wrote about this stark and impressive juxtaposition in these words, "With a businessman's President in the White House who kept telling us . . . that the system was perfectly sound . . . we wondered about the survival of republican American institutions; and we became more and more impressed by the achievement of the Soviet Union."

These are the main keys to an understanding of the attraction to communism not only of thousands of intellectuals and professionals, but of middle-class elements and hundreds of thousands of workers, as well. This disillusionment with capitalism and the awesome respect for the evident advances of Russia could hardly take the form of a swing to the socialist movement, let alone to the tiny Trotskyist movement. The latter had only assurances to offer of what they could achieve some time in the future; the Communists could offer the reality, or what seemed to be the reality, of the Russian present. On his return from Russia, Lincoln Steffens said, "I have seen the future and it works." The Communist party appeared as the authorized representative of a promising future which was already in the present and already working.

This factor was reinforced by others. Most important was the vehemently antifascist position that the Communist party now took under the new slogan of "a broad all-inclusive unity" of everybody against the horror of fascism. As Hitler consolidated and extended his power, and the nature of this power became unmistakable, all decent people recoiled in dread and worry from this new barbarism. And what group now appeared as the most reasonable, practicable, and tolerant champion of unity against the menace of fascism that it had so fiercely opposed in Germany before 1933? Why, the Communist party, here and elsewhere! Gone apparently was its dogmatism, its fanaticism, its virulence, its insistence on the acceptance of Communist doctrine. It was now ready to work with virtually anybody – non-Communists, even nonsocialists, even nonliberals – on the simple and elementary basis of defending democracy. It was vastly seductive.

Moreover there was the new growing Russian socialist state, a mighty economic and military power. And this power was a great, possibly the greatest force for peace and against Hitlerism. It was now for the League of Nations, for collective security, for nonaggression pacts, and for the defense of democracy. It was toning down or abandoning the disruptive utopia of world revolution, and subordinating its Communist dogmas to the preservation of world peace and democracy. It was ready to unite with all the democracies, despite their capitalist character, and had already made such an alliance with democratic republican France; or so it all seemed. What more could a reasonable person of good will ask for?

In addition, it was making good on its claims in real and vital fields of conflict, the most important of which was the civil war in Spain. The Communists were fighting most sacrificingly for Loyalist democracy, and against Franco. The Communists were even rejecting the ideas of a socialist republic in Spain in order to assure the broadest possible unity of all democrats in the war against fascism. And of all the great or little powers in the world, who but Russia, and only Russia, was sending arms to the beleaguered Loyalists who were fighting so valiantly against Franco, against Hitler, and against Mussolini?

Finally in the United States itself, a new popular movement exploded in the country that excited an almost unexampled enthusiasm and support from all radical and liberal forces. That was the formation and growth of the CIO, which rapidly swept millions into its ranks and which brought to terms for the first time in American history most of the industrial and monopolistic giants who had till then kept the big fortresses of open shop-ism unbreeched. With model energy, dedication, and skill, Communists flocked to the CIO movement and before long established themselves, also for the first time in their history, as a tremendous force in the labor movement. And the "Popular Front" policy, especially in its aspect of supporting Roosevelt and the New Deal, to which the great majority of the workers were committed, was admirably suited to facilitating wide and deep penetration of the new union movement.

This almost miraculous combination of forces and circumstances served to mushroom the Communist party in a very few years into the overwhelming force in American radicalism. It is no exaggeration to say that 95 per cent of the people who became radicals in that time became Communists or moved within the orbit of its leadership or influence.

The Trotskyists were perfectly well aware of the true origin and the true nature of Communist "Popular Front" policy. They knew perfectly well that its source lay entirely in the foreign policy needs of the Russian state; that it was dictated solely by the interests of this state as it saw them; that it had no genuine relationship with the needs and interests of democracy, let alone of socialism. But at that time it was impossible to convince more than a tiny and helpless minority. It was like trying to push back an avalanche with bare hands, or with logic and reason.

Yet, in the middle of 1936 it appeared that a change was beginning at the periphery of the Communist-dominated radicalism. The first of the Moscow Show Trials burst upon Russia and the world. The Trotskyists were then on the verge of undertaking their experiment of entering the Socialist party, where they remained for a brief but shattering two years. Better than anyone else, they knew the truth about the Trials and understood their meanings. They did not need to wait twenty years for Khrushchev's revelations about the Stalinist epoch. The Stalinists were engaged in consolidating a regime of totalitarian absolutism, and to achieve it virtually the entire pleiade of revolutionary leaders and militants who had led Bolshevism to its victory in 1917 and saved the revolution in the harsh days of the civil war and foreign intervention had to be destroyed—not only politically and morally but also physically.

The Trotskyists felt duty bound to come to the defense of the victims of this wholesale slaughter inaugurated by the Trials. The difficulties they encountered were almost unimaginable. And that alone is a tribute to what they managed to achieve. Bourgeois public opinion was generally hostile. Not necessarily because it felt that Stalin had justice on his side and the charges against the oppositionists and former oppositionists were true.

But on the whole, bourgeois opinion could be summed up in the phrase, "Let the Red Rabble kill each other off." The labor movement was indifferent largely because of its well-known disinterest in foreign affairs, especially at the time when it was overwhelmingly preoccupied with the task of organizing the CIO, and more especially because of the increased strength and authority of the Communists in their ranks who would violently resist any criticism of Moscow.

The liberals were up to their brows in "Popular Frontism." Criticism of Communists was muted; criticism of Russian Communists was entirely excluded. Undermine the faith of millions in the only power in the world that is fighting Hitlerism in Spain and Europe and throughout the world? Absolutely not! The traditional journals of American liberalism, *The Nation* and *The New Republic*, endorsed the Moscow Trials with only slightly less vigor and tenacity than did the Stalinists themselves. They endorsed them with arguments that are to the unexpugnable shame of the American liberals.

Stalin could not possibly have chosen more shrewdly the moment for the cruel massacre of his opponents. He protected himself from practically all possibility of effective protest and criticism by the policy of the "Popular Front," by his anti-Hitlerism, by his aid to the Spanish Loyalists, by his revolutionization of the Russian economy. Under that cover, it was easy to carry through the bloody purges, the massive liquidation of millions, the establishment of the unspeakable slave-labor camps, and the ruthless exploitation of the Russian workers and peasants.

Trotskyist criticism of the Trials could find only a restricted audience and an even more restricted group of supporters. This was the climate of the times, the climate of the intoxicating magic of "Popular Frontism," the climate of the grand illusion about Stalinist Russia. It was a time when all doubts about Russia were waved away by the then famous phrase (which is nowadays regaining popularity in another application, alas), "You can't make an omelet without breaking eggs." That sounded vastly convincing, since even an ignorant cook knows it to be irrefragably true. Few stopped to ask, "Whose eggs are they?" "What is happening to the hens?" "Who is cooking the omelet?" and above all, "Who is eating it?" Only a few stopped to point out: it is not eggs that are involved but people—men and women, human beings to whom socialism is to bring serenity, freedom, and abundance. It is not eggs, but millions whose human rights, whose democratic rights, whose liberty, and whose very lives are at stake.

This the Trotskyists said, and more. To their support came the golden idealist, Norman Thomas, and practically all the other socialists. So did the old anarchist leader in his country, Carlo Tresca. And so, above all others, did the grand dean of American academic thought, freedom, and progress, Dr. John Dewey. Even in his old, old age, out of his profound feeling for justice, Dewey agreed to serve as chairman of the commission that was established to investigate the charges against Leon Trotsky. The commission which, after exacting and scrupulous examination of all evidence, including a hearing of Trotsky himself in his last exile in Mexico, concluded that the charges against Trotsky were false, and that the Moscow Trials were a hideous fraud.

Like a few others, I spoke at meetings all over the country to tell the truth about the Trials in the hope of winning enough support from American radicals at least to modify the scope of the massacres in Russia. Only a few thousand who escaped the influence of Stalinism responded. The others were indifferent or clearly antagonistic. In Los Angeles, for example, some friends arranged a meeting for me to speak to Hollywood figures. The movie colony was at that time virtually inundated by Stalinist radicalism. It was like a fad – stars, directors, writers by the hundreds were in that sphere. Like their counterparts throughout the country, they were ready at every moment to speak out against an injustice in the United States and everywhere else in the world, to join protests, to sign petitions, to give financial aid – and to give it with a large and open hand. For the victims of Stalinist injustice, not a soul could be found to say a word. I went to the meeting reluctantly and my skepticsim was justified. Only a score of the Hollywood colony appeared and it is worth noting that they were almost all Europeans of distinction and of political sophistication acquired in their sympathetic contact with European radical and liberal movements. The native luminaries did not respond. They did not display the smallest interest or concern.

The most heartening response came from radical intellectuals. Intellectuals are divided, as I long ago had occasion to say, into three classes: the skilled intellectual, the semi-skilled intellectual, and the unskilled intellectual, like workers in general. Of the thousands who became radicals in the critical decade of the thirties, the overwhelming majority gravitated to the Communists. But the Moscow Trials became a sort of watershed among them. The bulk of them went along slavishly and uncritically, some of them disgracefully, with the persecutors, and curses against "Hitlero-Trotskyists" flowed from their lips and their typewriters. In the prevailing climate it took a great deal of integrity, intelligence, and courage to come out in Trotsky's defense or even in favor of a fair and impartial hearing of the Russian defendant.

It is gratifying to recall that among the skilled intellectuals many of the finest minds and talents, the warmest hearts, defied the abuse and the calumny heaped upon them by the Communists and joined in the defense of Trotsky's revolutionary honor, or at the very least, his right to be heard in his own name. They included men and women like James T. Farrell, Edmund Wilson, John Dos Passos, Max Eastman, Sidney Hook, Phillip Rahv, and William Phillips and Lionel Abel (the editors of *Partisan Review*, who at that time broke away from the Communists). Also Mary McCarthy, Suzanne La Follette, Ben Stolberg, Charles Yale Harrison, Meyer Schapiro, Lionel Trilling, James Rorty, James Burnham, John Chamberlain, Dwight MacDonald, and scores of others. It was the first large breech in the formerly tight wall of Communist and pro-Communist intellectuals. The controversies that followed among the radical intellectuals were exceedingly bitter. From that time onward it was no longer possible to effect a reconciliation between the Communist intellectuals, who were eventually reduced to a handful of unskilled and sterile writers, and the non-Communist intellectuals.

It was in the fight against the Moscow Trials, which occupied a good deal of the second half of the thirties, that so many American radical intellectuals learned to understand the modern communist state and movement.

They came to see that whatever its tactics and maneuvers of the day, whatever its postures and guises, it is the defender and beneficiary of a totalitarian despotism which has nothing in common with either democracy or socialism. Most of them became friendly to the Trotskyists; a few even joined their ranks. But even though none of them remained Trotskyists for long, they took this insight with them for the rest of their lives. So did others during this stormy period—men and women who are not to be classified as intellectuals. Still others gained this insight after the signing of the Hitler-Stalin Pact. And still others were to acquire it only after the sanguinary suppression of the Hungarian Revolution, years and years later.

If there is one man to be singled out as the individual who was the main source of this insight, this understanding, this cleansing of the struggle for democracy and socialism from the corroding blight of totalitarianism, that man is Trotsky. No movement that I know of was ever so dependent on a single leader for its ideas, its guidance, and its inspiration, as was the Trotskyist movement. However that may be judged, it is a fact. He may have erred in many ways, as indeed he did—in more ways, I believe, than today's Trotskyists might grant. And not everything he said or did has endured the unmerciful test of time. But no matter how severely critics may rate him, objectivity and fairness would compel a recognition of his gifts. He was the captain of the Bolshevik Revolution. Without any professional training, he was the creator and leader, and often the field commander of the Red Army in the early days. The theory and politics of Marxism was the home in which he was an easy master. He was probably the greatest orator of his time, certainly the greatest in the revolutionary movement. The muscular elegance of his literary gift was not equalled by anyone else in the ranks of the Marxists, whatever their school. The purity and wholeness of his commitment to the socialist ideal was unsurpassed and he was as unflagging in adversity, of which he had an ample share, as he was unaffected in victory.

Early in the days when the process began that transformed the liberating hopes of the revolution into the reality of the new tyranny, he took his stand against the recession without asking if it was popular or unpopular to do so, without making sure first of all that victory was guaranteed in advance, without concern for his personal fate. Against the rise of totalitarianism he planted his feet wide and stubbornly, never giving ground or bending his neck, fighting with open visor and with the weapons of his rich intellectual arsenal. Even after all his comrades had fallen or conceded to the enemy, even after he was driven from exile to exile on three continents he did not waver in his chosen battle until his last day, and then only when a blow split open his skull.

There have not been many figures like this in the political world of our century. It is no wonder then that his ideas and his struggles opened the minds and lifted the hearts of many of the best of a whole generation, young and old. The Trotskyists did not succeed in the thirties, or afterward, in becoming a real political force, as the Communists for a while did. But while Trotskyism did not create a political party, it did create a political school. And many learned their politics and their ideals in it. In studying in this school, in working in it, in fighting with it, there was much to learn. And if in later years, many found that some of it had to be unlearned, much of it proved nonetheless to be fructifying and durable; and it remained.

It would not be easy to find many of those who went through this school and fought its fight in the thirties who would express resentments or regrets. Justice Holmes once wrote: "A man should have a part in the passions and the actions of his time, at the peril of being judged not to have lived." Those of us who went through the thirties would subscribe heartily to these handsome words. We know how true they were then. You will surely understand me if I add that they are no less true of the sixties.

GERALD L. K. SMITH

The Huey Long Movement

Introduction by Rita James Simon

H. L. Mencken described Gerald L. K. Smith as "the gustiest and goriest, the deadliest and damnedest orator ever heard of on this or any other earth – the champion boob-bumper of all epochs."

Gerald Lyman Kenneth Smith was born about 1898 in Pardeeville, Wisconsin. His father was a preacher. His grandfather and great grandfather had been circuit-riding hellfire and brimstone preachers. Smith carried on the family tradition. After graduation from Valparaiso University he held pulpits at various churches in Indiana before receiving the "call" to a large and fashionable church in Shreveport, Louisiana. This was in 1928, the year Huey Long was practicing law in the same city. The friendship between Gerald L. K. Smith and Huey Long dated from that time.

Rita James Simon is an associate professor in the Sociology Department and the Institute of Communications Research, University of Illinois.

Six years later in 1934, Smith left his pulpit and devoted all his time to organizing and publicizing Huey Long's "Share Our Wealth" program. He traveled all over the country setting up "Share Our Wealth Clubs." He was generally recognized as Huey Long's chief lieutenant in this endeavor. After Long's assassination, Smith was "eased out" of the Long machine by Louisiana politicians who decided not to perpetuate the Long feud with Roosevelt and the National Democratic Committee.

Smith then turned his talents to the Townsend movement and soon became a staunch supporter of Dr. Townsend's plan for providing pensions to persons over sixty years old.

In the fall of 1936, he joined forces with Father Coughlin and Townsend in promoting the candidacy of Congressman William Lempke for President against Roosevelt and Landon. In a speech sponsored by Coughlin's National Union for Social Justice, Smith denounced the Roosevelt administration and claimed that his real mission was to see that the "red flag of bloody Russia" was not hoisted in place of the stars and stripes."

After Lempke's disastrous showing at the polls in November, 1936, the Union Party dissolved and a few months later Smith formerly launched "A Committee of One Million" which he described as "a nationalist front against Communism." In his capacity as head of the committee, Smith traveled all over the country attacking the labor movement and the administration's foreign policy, and advocating isolationism.

During the war, Smith edited a newsletter called "The Cross and the Flag." The newsletter warned of too much collaboration with our allies, Britain and the USSR, and advocated "one hundred per cent loyalty to the war effort, but complete islolation after the war."

Since 1945, Gerald L. K. Smith has lived in Los Angeles. He describes himself as: "for all practical purposes, the senior advisor and liaison contact for something over 1700 right-wing organizations."

To UNDERSTAND THE HUEY LONG MOVEMENT and the political techniques of Huey Long in relationship to the nation as such, one must understand the background which produced the Huey Long reaction. In this brief talk I will not deal with local politics except as it becomes necessary to orient you to the circumstances which produced the Huey Long that the world knew, or at least thought they knew.

No one should approach an analysis of Huey P. Long with the attitude that he was a buffoon. The morgues of the press must very generally be ignored except where the facts are obvious and serve to refresh the memory. To illustrate, William Howard Taft while Chief Justice of the Supreme Court said: "Huey P. Long is the most brilliant, competent and intelligent attorney to have appeared before me during my term as the Chief Justice of the Supreme Court."

The text of Huey Long's approach to the state of Louisiana is found in his words, "Louisiana is the last stand of the feudal lords." The status of most states in the nation prior to the advent of Huey Long was that of progress and modern advancement. Any backward or offensive symptoms in the social structure in states like Indiana, Illinois, etc., sank into insignificance compared to what prevailed in Louisiana. To summarize the situation in Louisiana would require a book. In this instance, we will confine ourselves to a brief outline:

1. Nearly half the children were not in school.

2. There were thirty miles of improved highway in the entire state.

3. No bridges spanned main rivers.
4. There was virtually no hospital service for the indigent, helpless, and impoverished.
5. The University of Louisiana used some ante-bellum buildings, now preserved as historic museums. Its educational rating was C and C-minus. A diploma from the University of Louisiana was virtually useless when presented to educational institutions of note and reputation.

The sophisticated and arrogant overlords of the state of Louisiana lived in New Orleans and the port area, quite as similar people lived in the metropolitan areas of the backward nations of South America. These overlords were very rich, very ruthless, and completely indifferent to the welfare of the general population. They elected and bought the state legislature under the supervision of a political machine in New Orleans known as "The Old Regulars." They journeyed into the inland as men of baronial wealth in Africa occasionally journey into the jungle.

The reader will observe that we use the terms plutocrat, baronial wealth, and monopoly overlords. The villains in the American economy, according to Huey Long, were not big businessmen who had attained their wealth by blood, sweat, and tears. The real villains were the barons and overlords who had come into plutocratic power by financial manipulations, monopolistic controls, and nonproductive economic chicanery. If he were alive today, Long would come to the defense of the independent, frugal, well-to-do businessman who is being squeezed out of the picture between the upper and nether millstones of state capitalism and plutocratic monopoly. He believed that monopoly was the mother of communism because, he said: "Should the Reds take over, all they need to do is make commissars out of the Rockefellers, the Mellons, and their ilk. They may liquidate the heads of the monopolies, but the organization would be ready-made and all they would need to do would be to appoint commissars in the place of the titular heads of the monopolies."

Disease was rampant and there were no public health facilities. A young doctor in Shreveport, Louisiana, who tried to start a health insurance program was dismissed from the medical association for unethical practice.

Second to New Orleans in the state was Shreveport. As a young man I was called to the pastorate of one of the most exclusive and distinguished churches of that city, where the officialdom was made up of the president of the Chamber of Commerce, the presidents of two banks, and the mayor of the city. There were some symptoms of modern improvements for the general masses, but not many. The most powerful official in the parish (and in Louisiana, the word "parish" is used as the word "county" is ordinarily used) was the sheriff. If a planter was having trouble with his help, the sheriff merely deputized the plantation owner as a deputy sheriff, and that settled everything. A stubborn employee could then be dealt with for having resisted an officer. This practice prevailed all over the state.

My separation from the organized church and my association with Huey Long is a story in itself. It did not represent a loss of faith, or a lack of faith. My belief in Christianity has grown through the years. It represented a belief that I was called for a unique purpose, and the explanation of the feelings which went through my heart and mind as I made this decision need not be discussed here. I was completely ostracized by the professional religionists who could not imagine a man being a Christian and a friend of Huey P. Long at the same time.

The French-populated area of Louisiana existed in a provincial charm similar to rural France. This population was completely Catholic. They were emotionally adjusted to their lot. Their destiny was placed in the hands of the priest and the local political leaders. Custom decreed that a Catholic (French Catholic) must always be lieutenant governor in the state of Louisiana.

Louisiana was covered with priceless virgin timber and it had literally billions of dollars worth of oil. The forests were being denuded, the gas wells were being drained, the oil was being pumped out, and nothing of this enormous wealth left for the people to demonstrate that it had ever been there.

Inconsiderate employers and baronial overlords would pay their helpers nothing. Then the depression struck and even the barons went broke. The planters were wiped out. The banks were menaced. Men of prominence and practical influence in every community stood in line for soup and handouts and whatever charitable dole was available during the term of Herbert Hoover. Many people forget that the pattern of bureaucratic welfare from the federal government was drawn up under Herbert Hoover. Many of our New Deal friends forget that one of the campaign slogans of Franklin D. Roosevelt was to put an end to Herbert Hoover extravagance and reduce the budget 25 per cent. One of Franklin D. Roosevelt's first acts of economy was to pull wounded and injured soldiers out of the veterans' hospitals via the notorious Economy Act, which resulted in many suicides and much unfavorable reaction.

Huey Long had sought the governorship twice, and if

he had been elected the first time he would have been too young to serve. He was defeated in the first attempt because of a downpour of rain which kept the country people from coming to the polls. He made many promises which few people believed that he could keep, but practically every promise was kept. They were not demagogic promises in the realm of unreality. They were honest, courageous promises that could be carried out if their proponent could stay alive.

To illustrate: A humble man and his wife had oil discovered on their property, but they could not sell it for the market price because they did not own a pipeline. In order to get their oil into the standard pipeline owned by the Standard Oil Co., they had to take whatever price they were offered, which was usually much less than the market price. Huey Long advocated that all pipelines should become common carriers and that a little man who discovered oil would not need to own a pipeline to get it on the standard pipeline any more than he needed to own a railroad to buy a ticket. This idea was very revolutionary and cost the big companies millions and millions of dollars in ill-gotten gain. It put murder in their hearts. This common carrier project was accomplished while Mr. Long was a railroad commissioner. (The Railroad Commission had full authority over oil and gas, etc.) The common carrier legislation popularized Huey Long and helped many humble men become modestly wealthy. The public often wondered how Huey Long got his campaign funds. Many of his campaign funds came from modestly rich men who would have been impoverished had Huey Long not whipped the Standard Oil Co. on the common carrier principle.

It must be remembered that the "Square Deal revolution" was organized after a processing tax of 5 cents per barrel had been put on Venezuela oil and other foreign produced oils. This threw the oil monopoly into a complete "tailspin" and it was compelled to start buying locally produced oil. Previously, Louisiana citizens who had discovered oil were not able to sell it because they could not compete with the oil produced with slave labor. The courageous gesture on the part of Mr. Long could easily account for the fact that modestly rich domestic oil men became his real friends. They supplied money for his campaigns and they made it possible for him to launch his nationwide movement without having to draw on a depression-impoverished public for blood-and-sweat donations as some of the other so-called reform movements had done.

When he became governor things began to happen. He built roads, schools, and hospitals. The "Old Regulars" in New Orleans were opposed to everything he stood for that was good for the people. It became necessary, he thought, to control the legislature by formulas similar to those which had been employed by the baronial overlords of New Orleans prior to his election. It must be admitted that members of the state legislature were brought under his influence by promises of favors. One time he openly confessed that he could win every battle in the state legislature except the battle against the United Gas Co. He said that their power to corrupt a lawmaker put the legislature beyond his reach in this matter.

Enemies, of course, spread the propaganda that Mr. Long was accumulating a vast fortune. This was false.

After he was assassinated, the family actually faced economic problems.

Many dramatic events took place during the governorship of Huey Long, which would require another book to discuss. Perhaps some day that book can be written; but one phase of the Long regime must not be overlooked. The hour came for banks to close. Texas lost something like 700 banks. Mississippi lost between 400 and 500 banks. Tennessee, Alabama, and states all over the nation lost banks by the thousands. Huey Long was not only cunning, sagacious, and instinctive, he was also brilliant, logical, and farsighted. (A study of Huey Long must not in any way be influenced by the conduct of any of his relatives in politics. Anyone by the name of Long in politics, including his son, Senator Russell Long, is as far removed from the capacities of the late Senator Huey P. Long as Franklin D. Roosevelt, Jr., is removed from Franklin D. Roosevelt, Sr.)

A new governor's mansion was built during Huey Long's term as governor. He invited all the bank officials of the state to be his guests at a banquet in the new mansion. A sumptuous dinner was served. Long arose from the table and said: "How did you like the dinner?" Everyone cheered and responded, some of them with oral acclaim, but as they looked up each door was occupied by well-armed state troopers. Long said: "Gentlemen, make yourselves at home. We have cots and beds in the rooms upstairs and we expect to be here for a few days." He thereupon called in his bank examiners, who in fact were already at the dinner, and made a complete survey of all the cash in all the banks, and then proceeded to call on the bankers to work out a formula for spreading this cash in the form of loans, etc., to the banks that were morally liquid, but frozen by the emergency. To make a long story short, only eleven banks in Louisiana were lost because of this bold strategy. It was pretty difficult to turn the depositors of those banks against Mr. Long after they had observed what happened to the depositors in other states where hundreds and thousands of banks were lost.

He was not a demagogic buffoon! It must be remembered that his political organization controlled the state until his death, and at his death Louisiana bonds topped the market in Wall Street.

Another dramatic incident was based on the fact that during the bank crisis he kept the telephone at his bedside and followed it like a fire chief during a phenomenal outbreak. He told every bank president to call him at any hour of the day or night if he faced a crisis. One day he received a call from a bank in western Louisiana, and the president said: "Huey, they are going to make a run on my bank tomorrow." Long replied: "Go down to the bank and stay there until I get there." In less than one hour and a half, he and the bank examiners were there. They went through the books to make sure that the bank had been honestly run. He had with him the proper authorities of the state to draw a check for the total deposit the state had in the bank, thus stripping it of all its cash. When opening time came the crowd gathered in front of the bank demanding their money. Mr. Long stepped out on the front steps, and they said: "Hello, Huey, what are you doing here?" He shocked them first by saying, "I came to make sure that the State of Louisiana got its money, but I put in some telephone calls," said Huey, "and we are going to have a whole planeload of money here in a little while. It is coming in from Dallas. How many would like to go with me out to the airport to get it?" He dramatized the situation. They went to the airport together, where the money was brought out in suitcases. Long opened them and showed the money to the crowd. After returning to town, he went into the bank, and when the money had been properly placed, he came out on the front steps of the bank and said to the crowd, "Come and get it. All you need is here." Some came in and got their money, but most of them turned away. Can you imagine how that crowd felt toward Huey Long?

He dramatized all of his activities. He was one of the few public officials who knew how to stay on page one of every section of the newspaper. To illustrate his general appeal to the public: During one of the football seasons the State University of Tennessee was in a critical bind financially. They needed one big game to pull them out. They petitioned and begged Huey Long to attend the game between Tennessee and Louisiana even though everyone knew it was to be one-sided and would ordinarily draw a small crowd. He did so and marched across the packed stadium with the Louisiana State University band. These gestures were publicized by the smearing press as exhibitions of arrogance, but they were in fact the activities of a man who understood the hearts of the American people. He was mobbed wherever he went, whether on Broadway in New York, or at an airport in Cleveland. No man in this generation has attracted the crowds that he attracted outside of a President of the United States or Charles Lindbergh after his historic flight.

He was a gourmet of distinction. His scientific understanding of football was uncanny. On one or two occasions he actually called the coach to where he was seated and gave him the scientific instruction necessary to win the game. This seemed like arrogance to some people, especially his enemies, but it looked pretty good to the great crowds who wanted to win the game, especially against the University of Tulane in New Orleans. The feud between Tulane and the University of Louisiana was not just a normal interuniversity feud. It was based on the fact that many of the outstanding alumni of Tulane as well as the officials of Tulane campaigned openly against all appropriations for the State University of Louisiana on the grounds that it would imperil the future of Tulane.

The nearest thing to an armed revolt which took place during the days of Huey Long occurred when officers inside the Standard Oil Co. organized a militia. They were armed with guns and assembled at the airport with instructions to march on the state capitol and conduct a coup d'etat. They were called the Square Deal Army. Such dramatic blunders on the part of the opposition pyramided Mr. Long's popularity. Those who would say that Huey Long became powerful and popular because of coercive practices patterned after the Kelly-Nash machine in Chicago or the Tammany Hall in New York are just not realistic in their understanding of the Huey Long regime. Huey Long was powerful because he was popular. His popularity was gained at great risk to himself, both physically and socially.

For instance, he was able to popularize the building of highways, but was having great difficulty in popularizing the need for a great state university. Millions of dollars had been raised for the highways, but the legislature, under pressure from the baronial interests, would not appropriate money for a great university. One day he called in his controlled highway commission and asked them to buy a rather unimportant piece of land from the state university for an exorbitant sum, which they did. That bold gesture was the foundation and the spearhead which resulted in the building of the University of Louisiana.

When Mr. Long ran for the United States Senate, forces scarcely imaginable were mobilized against him. His private secretary, Alice Grojean, was one of the finest, purest, and most wholesome young women who could be imagined. Her competency was unexcelled, and she was almost a genius in transcribing copy and taking dictation. Her first husband was a derelict and was addicted to dope and liquor. Someone hit upon the idea that it would defeat Huey Long's campaign for the United States Senate if he were sued for alienation of affection by the derelict husband of Alice Grojean. But there was a leak in the plan and two days before the election, just the day before the suit was to be filed, two men visited the hotel where Mr. Grojean was staying, walked him very politely to an airport, and put him in an airplane. He was kept up in the air until the night of the election. The New Orleans newspapers, which were in on the original plot, threw out an alarm and made a big issue of his disappearance. But on the night of the election Mr. Grojean was brought back and walked up to a microphone and told everybody that he was all right and that nothing had happened to him. An island out in the Gulf had been used as a landing field to come down for food, gasoline, etc. The "Old Regulars" of New Orleans had discovered that the man who could be bought for one price could be bought for a higher price. It is doubted that the scandal that would have been broken the day before the election could have defeated Mr. Long, but the plot symbolized the desperation of his enemies.

Huey Long went to Washington. In the meantime, the depression was deepening. Franklin Roosevelt was running for the Presidency. The vote at the Democratic party convention in Chicago had been close. It soon became obvious that Huey Long held the balance of power. He had influenced enough delegates to determine who should be nominated. He exerted his influence on the side of Franklin D. Roosevelt because he thought that Roosevelt would establish a regime in harmony with the philosophy that Huey Long had represented in Louisiana. However, he later broke completely with Roosevelt.

We will not take time to discuss the break, but Huey Long lived and died doubting that Franklin D. Roosevelt was a sincere, practical, realistic liberal. He believed that he was influenced by other forces that tended to antagonize responsible business without giving proper relief to the great masses.

In the meantime, the Marxists were busy. They presented themselves in every area as Trotskyites, Stalinites, Leninites, Norman Thomas Socialists, etc. As the outgrowth of a dramatic personal experience, I had joined hands with Huey Long and we were moving into the national scene. Along with others, we both became obsessed with a determination to defeat Franklin D. Roosevelt for re-election in 1936. But we knew that he could not be defeated by reactionaries such as Alf Landon. We believed that the imagination of the people must be captured in such a way as to outbid the emotional appeal of Franklin D. Roosevelt without imperiling the basic economy of the nation. Mr. Long felt that Mr. Roosevelt threatened the basic economy of private enterprise.

I have no boasts to make concerning anything I did for Huey Long. He was complete in himself, but he was honest enough to accept what he called wisdom from others. I gave him the basis for one of his favorite conversations with responsible businessmen, who were afraid of what they called his radicalism. It went something like this:

In the light of the present situation and in the light of the universal ballot, which will continue to become more universal, every election day must be Christmas Day for the rank and file voter. What does that mean? It means that the day after the election, the humble voter who does not understand the complexities of government must be able to reach up and take something off the Christmas tree because his side won. Gentlemen, if responsible people in this nation are not willing to pay that price for victory, then we will go down the valley into communism and dictatorship. To illustrate: The average conservative Democrat and the average Republican when he outlines his programs of balanced budgets, reminds me of a father who calls his family in the day before Christmas and says, "We are not going to indulge in anything as silly, as emotional, and as illogical as Christmas presents. I have a complete report here of the family budget, and it is balanced. I have broken the budget down and have pro-rated the cost of operating this household to every member of the family. I have caused a copy of this pro-ration to be written up on a piece of paper. For instance, Johnny, your pro-rata share in the family budget last year was $840.00. Here is a well-prepared copy of what it cost to keep you for a year. The bills are all paid. This represents the family contribution to you of more than $800.00. Here is my autograph, and you will notice at the bottom of the page the words 'Merry Christmas.'" Gentlemen, can you imagine any father holding the emotional respect of his children by that sort of behavior? No, he had better reduce the family budget a little and roll out a red bicycle, a doll that sleeps, a few boxes of candy and the ordinary trinkets of Christmas. If we who are responsible to the great unschooled masses cannot learn how to make elections as interesting to the voter as Christmas is to the child, then we had better prepare to be defeated by someone who does know how.

I believe that Lyndon Johnson thinks that he is an imitator of Huey Long. He was a great admirer of Huey Long. But I also believe that he has imitated the superficial characteristics of Huey Long without sensing the deeper implications of Long's philosophy.

Mr. Long's definition of practical statesmanship was: "The ability to campaign as convincingly as a demagogue with much of the drama of a demagogue while possessing an inner self-respect dedicated to Constitutional procedures and a high regard for the national tradition."

The press, which was mostly reactionary at that time, began to represent us as radicals, and we were waited on by all the international propagandists and organizers in the world. They came from everywhere—from Moscow, from New York, and from Washington, thinking that they could exploit these young radicals like Huey Long and Gerald Smith. In many instances we drew them out and looked in on their whole program of terror, revolution, and bids for power. The more we visited with people like this, the more we reacted against their formulas. Because we dared to fight the barons, we were called radicals and Communists, and because we repulsed the Communists and refused to permit their infiltration into our activities, we were represented to the world as fascists. Huey Long was held up by his Moscow enemies and their puppets in America as a would-be dictator. They overlooked the fact that he repulsed the Ku Klux Klan ruthlessly. He refused to receive any representative of the German Nazi regime, and he refused to permit himself to be exploited by the international Communist machine.

These were all ideological conflicts, which did not endanger his life. The thing that really endangered his life was the fact that he was dethroning the barons of Louisiana and threatening the national and international barons, who, strangely enough, were political cohorts of Franklin D. Roosevelt. That is one thing that the superficial observer usually overlooks. All of the liberals who were liberal in the tradition of Constitutional government were on the side of Huey Long in Louisiana. All the baronial overlords who had enslaved the state right down to the days of Huey Long were in the Roosevelt machine.

What could Huey Long say to out-dramatize Franklin D. Roosevelt, who was a cunning demagogue in the eyes of his enemies and a progressive statesman in the eyes of his friends? Huey Long hit upon the contagious words "share our wealth." He thus discussed the high concentrations of wealth and said that we would never have real prosperity in America until these baronial empires were siphoned out into the economy. It makes one smile in a day like this to be reminded that Huey Long had said: "no man should be allowed to accumulate a personal fortune of more than five million dollars without heavy taxation." Can you imagine how many big American businessmen today would hope that anything as unradical as that would prevail in our economy at this moment?

When Huey Long talked about "share our wealth," he did not have in mind a "Robin Hood" program that would take and give, but he had in mind a program which would limit exploitation so that the great natural wealth of his state and nation would be made available to build schools and roads and produce an environment for health and development."

"Share our wealth" was defined in many ways by Mr. Long, such as, "The bowels of the earth are filled with oil and gas and minerals. The face is covered with forests and natural resources. When these are extracted from the ground they should leave on the top of the ground blessings to speak for the resources that have been taken. The blessings should include schools, hospitals, etc."

Suffice it to say, he had the kind of voice that people could not resist. His mail was phenomenal. When the mail came into Washington, D.C., one truck took the mail to all the United States senators except Huey Long. Another truck carried only mail to Huey Long. His mail was heavier than the White House mail, and his popularity grew to the point where a shrewd politician like James A. Farley was able to say: "If Huey Long had lived, he could have been elected President in 1936."

The "Share Our Wealth" movement spread like a prairie fire, and the number of those writing for free information became so enormous that at one time it required twenty-five people just to open the mail and classify it, not counting those it took to answer it and fulfill the requests of the people. It makes Lyndon Johnson look a bit antiquated when we reflect on the fact that the first tract which went out concerning the "Share the Wealth" movement specified that an economy should be developed which would make it impossible for any individual to possess less than $5,000.00 worth of property. This was the "red bicycle" in front of the Christmas tree, and what it did to influence the thinking of the great rank and file can scarcely be imagined. Nothing has happened like it since.

Organizational techniques for the "Share Our Wealth" Society were simple. An individual would hear a speech on the radio by Huey Long and write him a letter. Long would then send him a big broadside circular summarizing the five simple principles for the redistribution of wealth based on sound economy and Constitutional procedures. Mr. Long was opposed to a discussion of theory and detail because he said: "When economics are discussed every disciple has a different theory. This breeds division and destroys the practical techniques of the political strategy necessary to attain power required for reform."

Each spokesman was urged to form a local "Share Our Wealth" Society with the understanding that it could meet in the home and not have a treasury. Facetiously Huey would frequently say: "Most organizations are broken up by the treasurer running away with the money." He said that it should require no expense for a man to invite ten people to meet in his home. Furthermore, this encouraged small organizations, too small to trade off the organization and too small to trade off the enterprise to a political foe.

This was a very deceptive strategy in dealing with the opposition, because if a little community of two thousand people had fifteen or twenty "Share Our Wealth" societies, they were usually not too conscious of each other. At least one of them would always be formed by the opposition so that the organization could be sold out in return for a post office, or a bridge, or a federal job. But when the deal was made the opposition found out that they had only bought one of perhaps thirty-three organizations in the community. The sale had been made, but nothing had been bought of consequence. This completely confounded the opposition. These little groups sprang up literally by the thousands in the United States. It was estimated that there were at least a hundred thousand little "Share Our Wealth" societies covering the forty-eight states at the time of Long's assassination.

In the meantime, Long was represented in the reactionary press as a buffoon, a lunatic, a fascist, a Communist, a demagogue, and what have you. It did not seem to upset the people. Everywhere he went he was met by thousands upon thousands. It was a case of complete and genuine popularity, because Huey Long had no patronage outside of the state of Louisiana. His popularity in California, Maine, New York, Chicago, etc., could not be related to the fact that he came into a community and brought millions of dollars to abolish poverty or some ordinary political handout. He was admired, he was loved, he was believed in, and the great rank and file instinctively knew that he was their friend.

The behavior of the robber barons and those who had exploited the nation's wealth beyond any of the decencies of private enterprise was responsible for this reaction. About this time a great industrialist in Indianapolis had allowed himself to be quoted nationally, "I hope the day will come when workingmen have to go to church in overalls and the maximum wage will be a dollar a day." In the automobile shops at Detroit, gangsters were being hired as foremen. Any man caught working slowly or doing less than he was supposed to do was frequently struck and knocked down beside the bench. It was Huey Long's belief that these people could be rescued from industrial and political tyranny in a Constitutional manner.

Unfortunately, the pain of the persecuted and the suffering of the downtrodden were exploited by opportunistic radicals who came to us from other lands, or who sent philosophies to us from other lands. The same technique was employed then as is being employed today in the civil rights movement. The whole movement is being imperiled by the kibbitzers, the interlopers, the opportunists, the agents of self-interest who enjoy fishing in troubled waters.

It was not generally known, but one of Senator Long's greatest admirers was the late Henry Ford, the great industrialist. He believed in "Sharing Our Wealth" by practicing sound economy. He was even opposed to charity, saying that charity should not be necessary. Wages and opportunities should be made so completely available to the rank and file that the only charity which should be necessary should be for the completely indigent who had never been given any opportunity to save or profit by their skills. Reverses of this philosophy were introduced into the Ford Motor Co. after Mr. Ford aged so that he was unable to determine the course of the company he had founded. I found in Mr. Ford a great friend, and the story of my relationship to him is another story.

It would be interesting to posterity to know the men of wealth and influence who introduced themselves to me and expressed an understanding conviction concerning the political techniques and the philosophical practices of those of us who were the directors of the Huey Long movement – Huey Long being the chief philosopher and the chief intellect. To represent one's self as a member of Huey Long's brain trust would be false in the extreme. He was his own brain trust. He was one of the few prominent men that I have known, and I have known hundreds in my dramatic lifetime, who commanded my complete respect. This is not an appraisal of his personal life. In dealing with the personal limitations of a human being, it is well for us to remember the admonition of the One who said: "Judge not, lest ye also be judged, for with what measure ye judge, ye shall be judged."

It is my belief and the belief of some of us who have been branded as reactionaries that genuine progress and sincere development in this country has been hindered by the infiltrators who pose as the people's friends, but are in fact the people's enemies. Huey Long was a *real* friend of the people.

He believed that most public officials and politicians were too dishonest to be realistic and too sanctimonious and self-righteous to face reality. Instead of conducting themselves in such a way as to inspire the confidence of the multitude, they usually flattered the multitude by making the most complete ignoramus in the community think that he was an intellectual. It was Mr. Long's assumption that we must recognize at the outset that a large majority of the voters are not capable of thinking out solutions to the nation's problems scientifically and philosophically. On election day the people vote to satisfy their little whims of support and opposition. If they give victory to a traitor, or a charlatan, or a complete demagogue, then they have given away their country. America's tradition, said Huey Long, was built around George Washington, and his compatriots. But when George Washington was elected only one adult out of twenty-five could qualify to vote. Only people with a sense of responsibility could qualify. Now that millions of unenlightened people are qualified to vote, said Mr. Long, we must learn how to reach their minds and mobilize them in the most constructive way possible. He did not believe in the limited vote. He was one of the first leaders to advocate repeal of the poll tax. The abolition of the poll tax in Louisiana took place during the lifetime of Huey Long.

Huey Long was a man of great faith, but he was quite cynical concerning the dependability of certain professional religionists. When he attempted to clean out the brothels of New Orleans (which had always been an impossible undertaking) he was opposed by the ministerial association as well as the "Old Regulars." In an outburst of frankness he said: "When you are in a pinch, the whore houses and the preachers are always on the same side." This was not said in a blasphemous mood, because he had a deep and high regard for the Christian faith.

Speaking of religion, one of his most intelligent and cunning projects was the introduction of free school books into the parochial schools of Louisiana. He was very much in favor of free school books for all schools, both public and parochial, because the Catholic Church in Louisiana had been carrying about one-third of the educational load until the advent of Huey Long. Many communities would scarcely have had schools had it not been for the Catholic Church. When he promised free school books to the Catholic schools, he was fought both by the plutocratic barons of wealth and the anti-Catholic bigots. His native church was the Baptist Church, and he almost lost his "amateur standing" in the Baptist Church by proposing free school books for parochial schools. The matter was carried to the Supreme Court of the United States. Long wrote a one-page brief which said in essence: "We are not giving the school books to the schools; we are giving the school books to the children, and they have a right to carry those school books into any building designated by their parents." The court decided in his favor.

Never overlook the fact that when any effort was made to defeat Huey Long, or his organization, or his purposes, or his legislation, the baronial elements always had the cooperation of the Roosevelt administration and other shifty groups.

Because of his outspoken attacks on the regime and the accusation that Roosevelt was trying to out-Hoover Hoover by reducing the budget 25 per cent, Huey Long became a political outcast in the Roosevelt administration and lost all of his patronage. This increased his popularity in Louisiana, because the patronage went over to the "Old Regulars" and whenever a political job opened up, one hundred people wanted it, but only one could get it. That made ninety-nine people angry. Huey Long was cunning enough to sense that this would help him instead of hurt him.

Finally the pressure of Huey Long's popularity became effective in Washington. Mr. Roosevelt, in our opinion, began to introduce slogans and appeals in virtual imitation of Huey Long. Roosevelt spoke so convincingly at one time that Mr. Long rose on the floor of the Senate and boasted that Roosevelt was about to embrace his program. Later this opinion was cancelled out by other statements made by the President.

On the 9th of August, 1935, Huey Long rose on the floor of the United States Senate and prophesied his own assassination. He inserted into the senatorial record a dictaphone account of a meeting which had been held in New Orleans in which his assassination had been planned. This was represented to the world as a dramatic attempt to get attention and sympathy. But almost one month from the date of his announcement he and I were walking through the legislative chambers of the state capitol of Louisiana. We were approached by a young man who dashed out from behind a marble pillar and shot Mr. Long through the abdomen. He then turned his gun toward me. In that split instant, the assassin was shot down by the bodyguards. Senator Long was rushed to the Lady of the Lake Hospital behind the new beautiful state capitol of Louisiana. Two days later he died in my arms.

I delivered the funeral oration over his grave to the largest public funeral in American history. There were two hundred and fifty thousand people on the grounds. Three acres of land were required to hold the floral bouquets, which were laid down on the grass side by side. Bridges across the Mississippi River had not been completed and cars were backed up eight miles waiting to cross on the ferries.

In the meantime, two other popular movements had grown up in the United States, the Townsend movement and the Coughlin movement. Huey Long had had a few practical contacts with Townsend and Father

Coughlin, but they had not matured. It was understood that we would try to develop these followings in favor of a great insurgency that would elect Huey Long President. If we could not elect Long President, it would permit us to name the candidate on the Republican ticket. One of Huey Long's favorites was Senator William E. Borah of Idaho.

Republican strategists who came to Long thinking they could use him were told that he would be only too happy to cooperate in the defeat of Roosevelt, but they must run the risk of his (Huey Long) being elected. He refused to dissipate his own campaign just to split Roosevelt's following. James Farley believed that Long's campaign would have done more than split the Roosevelt vote. It could very easily have elected him.

I was represented to the nation as the leader of the Huey Long following in national politics, and I was very influential in Louisiana. I was one of nine men in control of the Louisiana organization. Suffice it to say that as we approached the 1936 national convention (after the Louisiana election had been held, in which every man elected to office was elected "on the blood of Huey Long") members of the President's cabinet and representatives of the Attorney General came to Louisiana and announced that they were preparing to press charges for income tax evasion against practically all of the influential members of the Huey Long organization except Gerald L. K. Smith. They intimated that a settlement could be arranged if the delegation to the Philadelphia convention aligned itself in favor of the administration. They not only intimated, they made it very clear.

For instance, a member of the President's cabinet told us that something like 500 million dollars had been earmarked for Louisiana for public development, but could not be released as long as the Long organization was in power. But if it became generally known that the Long organization had gone over to Roosevelt, officially, in 1936, these sums would start to flow – millions upon millions. The greedy men who had sold the blood of their mentor knew no restraint. They immediately began to develop great fortunes out of the sums which were released.

I rose and told the meeting that there was nothing they had that I wanted. I also told them that I did not propose to trade off the blood of the man from whose wet grave I had been catapulted into prominence. I later took all of the modest savings that I had and bought a complete radio hookup for the state of Louisiana from 9 P.M. to midnight in which I outlined the whole situation and the sellout. Following the address I was seized by the police of the City of New Orleans and thrown into jail together with my compatriots. I had not only been on the air, but I had addressed 70,000 people in the Plaza. There I stood, repudiated by the Long organization which had sold out completely to Roosevelt. To the stranger I was an associate of Huey Long; to the political gang which sold out, I was an outcast. I retired from the scene, penniless but in possession of man's greatest earthly gift – self-respect.

This experience recalled a visit that I had had with Mr. Long in the Crest Room of the state capitol. This room was a conference room that Mr. Long would use when he returned from Washington. We were sitting in a circle. He always referred to me as Dr. Smith. As he looked around at his leaders, he said: "God pity Louisiana. If anything ever happens to me, everyone in this room will go to jail except Dr. Smith." His prophecy was fulfilled later.

The Democratic convention met in Philadelphia, and the people who had been elected on the blood of Huey Long delivered the delegation to the Roosevelt forces. I was the maverick. Representatives of Dr. Townsend and of Father Coughlin came to me, and we joined hands.

The politicians in power were persecuting Dr. Townsend. We did not accept the economics of Townsend's plan completely, but he was a sincere friend of the people. He did not racketeer on the sentiments of the old people. He lived in a modest home, was economical in his personal habits, and the passion of his life was to bring security to the aged. A congressional committee of reactionaries announced an investigation. He was called to appear. It was a big thing, a full-dress, highly publicized campaign to bury, annihilate, and do a "snow job" on old Dr. Townsend. He was a relative stranger to me but I went to see him. He was encouraged by my visit. I was youthful, vital, and strong physically and fearless to the point of abandon.

He said to me: "What would you do?" I said: "I would hold myself in contempt of the committee."

"How?" he said.

I said: "Tomorrow when they meet [they had already been in session several days] read a brief statement to them, then turn around and walk out. I will lead you out. Then wait for the Committee to try to imprison you, and from behind prison bars you can determine the votes of ten million people."

He took my advice literally, and when he turned to walk out I was there. I grabbed his arm. (The morgues of the press show this picture. Offhand I remember that it appeared on page one of the *New York Times.*) Down the steps we went, and where do you think we went? We took a taxicab to Baltimore and to the residence of a man who was a friend both of mine and of Dr. Townsend's — H. L. Mencken. I am not saying that he was our friend because he was ideologically in agreement with us, but he was hungry for drama, individuality, and the guts of resistance. This gesture made the Townsend movement, which became the mother of old-age security in the United States.

The drama of this event inspired the interest of Father Charles Coughlin, and his personal representatives came to me and asked me to address his convention in Cleveland, Ohio, which I did. Not only did I address it, and not only did I address Townsend's convention, but when Father Coughlin was stricken ill I spoke in his place at the big closing session in the baseball stadium at Cleveland.

The popular uprising represented by the Farmers' Holiday Association, the Townsend movement, the Coughlin movement, and the Huey Long movement was, of course, frustrated by the assassination of Huey Long. The killers of Huey Long knew what they were doing. The true story concerning this event has never been told because other than myself the only public figures who know the true story are those who sold out and those who hated him. I have written this story with the understanding that it be released after my death, when the truth, which is so dangerous, cannot injure my loved ones. Too many guilty people are still alive.

The people I met during the summer of 1936 were all amateurs compared to Huey Long. The movement was awkwardly handled. Under the domination of Father Coughlin, a colorless, inadequate little fellow by the name of Congressman William Lempke was chosen as the presidential candidate. Landon was nominated by the Republicans. Lempke was nominated by the Union Party, which was the party of the "populace movements." The results, of course, were catastrophically victorious for Franklin D. Roosevelt.

The above is not the full story; it is merely a segment of the full story. But it is hoped that it will be of interest to the keepers of the archives and the preservers of tradition who realize that 1936 and the middle 1930's in general constituted one of the most dramatic periods in American political history.

Postscript: Huey Long believed, as most professional politicians know, that Franklin D. Roosevelt could not have been nominated at Chicago in 1932 without him. He believed sincerely that Roosevelt was jealous of him and that he was double-crossed by Roosevelt. This introduced an animosity that approached bloodshed, and regardless of the motivating force which brought it about, it resulted in bloodshed. It cannot be proved that Roosevelt ordered the assassination of Huey Long, but it can be proved that those who discussed his assassination were positively of the opinion that it would please the President.

GRANVILLE HICKS

Writers in the Thirties

Introduction by Theodore Peterson

In the 1930's, the far left had a big attraction for many writers. "For one thing," as Daniel Aaron has remarked, "it meant the end of romantic dichotomies; art and life, intellectual and Philistine, poetry and science, contemplation and action, literature and propaganda." For another thing, the Hoovervilles and farm foreclosures, the bread lines and the sleepers-in-doorways, represented not the aberrations of society. For a good many writers, then, Marx had preached the gospel, and the Soviet Union was the promised land.

Granville Hicks, writer and critic, well understands that leftward movement for he was a part of it. In 1932 he was a recent convert to Communism—a new type of convert, since he came from native New England stock. Mr. Hicks told of his conversion in a symposium in *New Masses*. He had come from Harvard, he said, as a "fairly typical liberal

Theodore Peterson is the dean of the College of Journalism and Communications, University of Illinois.

with a mild interest in socialism, a strong faith in pacifism, and the usual conviction that the desired changes in the social order could be brought about by the dissemination of sound ideas." The Sacco-Vanzetti case, he wrote, "crushed my faith in liberalism." The decay of the capitalistic system and long conversations with Communist friends enabled him, as he then put it, "to break through the fog of self-delusion and confusion."

Mr. Hicks was on the editorial staff of *New Masses* from 1934 to 1939. He became a card-carrying Communist in the winter of 1934–35; indeed, he once was invited to become educational director of the party. He remained a party member until the German-Soviet nonaggression pact, when, like many intellectuals, he broke in disillusionment.

His first book was *The Great Tradition: An Interpretation of American Literature Since the Civil War*, which appeared in 1933 and which was written while he was under the spell of Marxism. His most recent is an autobiography, *Part of the Truth*, which was published this year and which obviously was written while under no spell of bitterness and rancor. Between those two volumes, he has written a shelfful of other books, fiction and nonfiction, among them *John Reed: The Making of a Revolutionary*, which *Current History* chose as one of the ten most distinguished nonfiction works published in 1936.

Mr. Hicks was literary consultant to the anti-Communist *New Leader* from 1951 to 1958 and has been a contributing editor of the non-Communist *Saturday Review* since 1958.

He earned both his A.B. and A.M. at Harvard. He has taught literature at Smith and at Rensselaer Polytechnic Institute. He was counsellor on American civilization at Harvard in the 1938–39 academic year, and he has attributed his one-year contract to his political activities.

Since his days at Rensselaer, he has lived in an old farmhouse in Grafton, New York. He is very much a part of that little town, and is a leader in community affairs.

ONE CANNOT UNDERSTAND THE LITERATURE of the thirties without understanding the literature of the twenties. The twenties was a decade of revolt in literature and, indeed, in all the arts. We have always had a tradition of revolt, and I trust that we always will, but there was something special about the outburst at the end of the First World War. A cultural pattern was breaking up—the war itself was partly but not exclusively responsible for that—and the resulting sense of freedom was like strong drink.

The most convenient name for the pattern that was falling apart is Victorianism. Its conspicuous quality was prudishness, an excessive reticence with regard to sexual matters and bodily functions in general. But it was also marked by conventionally good manners, a superficial piety, and a polite conservatism in politics.

Victorianism was a calamity for writers: there were hundreds of subjects that could not be touched, scores of words that could not be used. Although there were societies for the suppression of vice, they were scarcely necessary, for most publishers were scared to death of violating any of the taboos. Major writers, as they always have done, found ways of saying what they wanted to say, of telling the truth as they saw it, but they constantly suffered from their lack of freedom.

The struggle against Victorianism had begun long before the First World War, but the victory came with a rush in the early twenties. One of the early fighters and one of those who best enjoyed the fruits of victory was H. L. Mencken, reporter, critic, and humorist. After helping for some years to edit a magazine called the *Smart Set*, he founded his own journal, the *American Mercury*, which became in many ways the epitome of the twenties. Mencken's method of attack was to make fun of everything, and he wrote with enormous vigor and sometimes with real wit. He ridiculed reformers – "wowsers" he called them – prohibitionists, Rotarians, Bible Belt preachers, sentimental novelists, prudish critics, hypocritical politicians, all sorts of people. And he had a lot of fun doing it. Here is a paragraph from a piece written in 1931 about the Presidency:

> The honors that are heaped upon a President are seldom of a kind to impress and content a civilized man. People send him turkeys, opossums, pieces of wood from the *Constitution*, goldfish, carved peach kernels, models of the state capitols of Wyoming and Arkansas, and pressed flowers from the Holy Land. Once a year some hunter in Montana or Idaho sends him 20 pounds of bear-steak, usually collect. It arrives in a high state, and has to be fed to the White House dog. He receives 20 or 30 chain-prayer letters every day and fair copies of 40 or 50 sets of verse. Colored clergymen send him illustrated Bibles, madstones and boxes of lucky powders, usually accompanied by applications for appointment as collector of customs at New Orleans, Mobile or Wilmington, N.C., or as Register of the Treasury. His public rewards come in the form of LL.D.'s from colleges eager for the publicity – and on the same day others precisely like it are given to a champion lawn-tennis player, a banker known to be without heirs of his body, and a General in the army. No one ever thinks to give him any other academic honor; he is never made a Litt.D., a D.D., an S.T.D., a D.D.S., or a J.U.D., but always an LL.D. Dr. Hoover, to date, has 30 or 40 such degrees. He apparently knows as little about law as a court catchpoll, but he is more solidly *legum doctor* than Blackstone or Pufendorf.[1]

What Mencken was doing was leading a revolt against American middle-class culture, which had two aspects –

[1] H. L. Mencken, Jr., *The American Scene* (New York: Alfred A. Knopf, Inc., 1965), pp. 223–224.

the Victorianism of which I have spoken and a high regard for business success. At the time it seemed that almost every writer of any talent was engaged in the same endeavor. Van Wyck Brooks was announcing the cultural bankruptcy of a business civilization, and he was supported by such men as Lewis Mumford and Waldo Frank. Sinclair Lewis poked fun at businessmen in *Babbitt*, and satirized a hypocritical evangelist in *Elmer Gantry*. In *Winesburg, Ohio* Sherwood Anderson suggested that life in the American small town was not so idyllic as had been generally supposed. Theodore Dreiser, in *An American Tragedy*, raised fundamental questions about American justice and American values. And there were countless lesser writers who were hitting out at any head they could find handy.

I can hardly exaggerate the animation with which the onslaught was conducted. In 1922 a man named Harold Stearns edited a volume called *Civilization in the United States*, with essays on such subjects as politics, the law, education, music, the literary life, and so on. It would be untrue to say that none of the contributors found anything good to report, but the upshot of the book was pretty dismal. Stearns himself decided that there was no civilization in the United States and went to live in Europe.

So did many other young Americans, for this was the great decade of the expatriates. As Malcolm Cowley pointed out in his *Exile's Return*, and as Morley Callaghan has reminded us in *That Summer in Paris*, countless Americans believed that great art could be created only on the other side of the Atlantic.

The young writers who sprang up early in the twenties seemed to be part of the same revolt. F. Scott Fitzgerald in *This Side of Paradise* (1920) announced that a new generation of college students had abandoned the standards of its parents. John Dos Passos' *Three Soldiers* (1921) attacked the values for which the First World War had supposedly been fought. Ernest Hemingway's first collection of short stories, *In Our Time* (1925), contained grim indictments both of the war and of the peace that followed it.

There is a paradox that must be grasped: much of the literature written in the twenties was somber and even tragic, but the spirit of the decade was one of exhilaration. I will let Dos Passos illustrate the point for me. *Three Soldiers* is a black novel, denounced in its own time as a vile misrepresentation of the spirit of the men who fought in World War I. Portraying three more or less representative young Americans, it carries each of them to his doom, and is intended to emphasize the horror and waste of war. Yet what was Dos Passos' mood when he wrote it? A dozen years later, in his introduction to the Modern Library edition, he described the spring of 1919:

> Any spring is a time of overturn, but then Lenin was alive, the Seattle general strike had seemed the beginning of the flood instead of the beginning of the ebb. Americans in Paris were groggy with theatre and painting and music; Picasso was to rebuild the eye, Stravinsky was cramming the Russian steppes into our ears, currents of energy seemed bursting out everywhere as young guys climbed out of their uniforms, imperial America was all shiny with the new idea of Ritz, in every direction the countries of the world stretched out starving and angry, ready for anything turbulent and new, whenever you went to the movies you saw Charlie Chaplin.[2]

[2] John Dos Passos, *Three Soldiers* (New York: George H. Doran, 1921).

"Ready for anything turbulent and new"—that was the way the world seemed to the young Dos Passos in 1919. It was a time of upheaval, and for the young, it was for that reason a time of hope. Heaven knew there was plenty wrong with the world; it was in a dreadful state. But the old tyrants were falling, the old barriers were collapsing, and anything could happen. Meanwhile there were large opportunities for raising hell.

For the most part, literary and artistic people in the twenties were not directly interested in politics; they did not join parties, even the left-wing parties, and they did not get up on soap boxes. But almost without exception they were against the status quo, against the regimes of Harding, Coolidge, and Hoover. And they felt that anyone else who was against the status quo was on their side.

In 1922, as a junior in college, I was a member of the Harvard Liberal Club, which had a series of luncheon speakers. I remember a single taxer, an anarchist, a vegetarian, a disciple of Gandhi, a Communist, several varieties of socialists, a representative of the British Labor party, an authority on adult education, an advocate of birth control, and so forth and so on, lunch after lunch. We would listen to anyone who was against the government. Needless to say, we did not agree with all of the speakers; we could not have, for often they were at one another's throats. We were quite aware that some of them were crackpots. But still we felt that in some sense they were all on our side.

Another thing to remember about the twenties is that, after a brief postwar depression, it was a decade of unusual prosperity. Big business and what we thought of as its government seemed absolutely impregnable. And most of us were in one way or another beneficiaries of national prosperity. How was H. L. Mencken able to publish a flossy journal such as the *American Mercury*? Because the publishing business of Alfred A. Knopf, Inc., was flourishing. How were the expatriates able to live abroad? Because they were taking advantage of a favorable rate of exchange. Why did I get a raise in salary at Smith College? Because papas were able to pay increased tuition fees.

Then the depression came. It began, of course, with the stock market crash of October, 1929, but our awareness of it did not begin then. I had started teaching that fall at Rensselaer Polytechnic Institute, and one or two of my colleagues got squeezed, but I thought it served them right for playing the market. After all, they still had their jobs, and their families woud not starve. Some of the big operators had been badly hurt, and a few committed suicide, but we had no great sympathy for the men of Wall Street. This, we said to ourselves, was what a business civilization was like.

But as 1930 went by, we began to wonder what was happening, and in 1932 it seemed clear to some of us that this business civilization that we had been belaboring on cultural and moral grounds had collapsed. The machines – those wonderful machines that had given so many of us a high standard of living – had stopped running. And more and more people were out of jobs. By 1932 some economists said that as many as 17 million people were unemployed, and that meant that every fourth person we met was jobless. And that probably meant that he and his family were suffering, for there was no unemployment insurance, and a man had nothing to fall back on but his own savings and whatever meager help his relatives could give him. We saw them on the street, the unemployed who were getting by, wandering hopelessly in search of work or standing dazed and bewildered on street corners. Those who were not getting by we saw sleeping on the stairs of subway entrances, covered with salvaged newspapers. Outside each city of any size, on some dump or other deserted area, was what was called a Hooverville – a colony of shacks made of odds and ends of tin and cardboard and burlap, in some of which whole families were living.

I was one of the lucky ones, for I had a job in the bad years; but my father lost his job, and he and my mother moved in with us. Everybody in the middle class, however lucky he may have been himself, knew someone – and, if he had any compassion, was helping someone – who was less fortunate. Everyone knew that something had to be done.

In the twenties, as I have said, few writers were political in any very specific sense. (There were some exceptions.) By 1931, however, more and more writers were saying that they had a responsibility for the state of the nation. After all, they had emphatically and sometimes stridently called attention to the shortcomings of our business civilization, and, now that that civilization had come close to collapse, they could not pretend that it was no business of theirs.

It may help you to understand what happened if you remember that artists are not temperamentally inclined to moderation. They aren't likely to say, "Oh, let's give a little here, and change a little there, and tinker with this and play around with that." They are, for better or for worse, more likely to demand that something fundamental be done and be done here and now. And to many writers in 1932 nothing seemed more fundamental than the program of the Communist party.

Like several of my friends in the twenties, I had considered myself a socialist with a small s, and I had supported Norman Thomas in the 1928 election. But in the crisis of the early thirties, socialism seemed too mild and ineffectual. John Dos Passos said that becoming a socialist would be like drinking near beer. We did not know so much about communism then as many of us have learned since, and the communists seemed to us different from other critics of the status quo only insofar as they were more realistic and more determined.

Many writers, as I have said, were beginning to ask themselves whether communism was not the answer, and in the summer of 1932 more than fifty of them signed a manifesto supporting the Communist candidates in the coming election. Many of the names would not be familiar to you, but some of them may be: Sherwood Anderson, Erskine Caldwell, Malcolm Cowley, Countee Cullen, John Dos Passos, Waldo Frank, Sidney Hook, Sidney Howard, Lincoln Steffens, Edmund Wilson. And my name was there too.

The case of Lincoln Steffens may be instructive. Older than most of us, he had won a great reputation as a muckraker between 1900 and 1910. Unlike most of the muckrakers, who were satisfied with bringing about particular reforms, Steffens was always probing, always trying to find out why things happened as they did. As time went on and the muckraking movement went out of fashion, his name became less and less well known, but he was still asking himself questions, and in the twenties he began writing his autobiography, which he tentatively called *My Life of Unlearning*. If the book had appeared in the prosperous twenties, it might have attracted little attention, but it was published in 1931, and in the depression years it seemed to many people, and particularly to many young people, to explain the world in which they were living.

Steffens was not a communist when he wrote the autobiography; although he believed that communism was working in Russia, he also believed that the new capitalism, so-called, was working in the United States and, for that matter, fascism was working in Italy. But then came the depression. "I went to New York," he wrote in one of his many letters to students, "to hear the semi-scientific captains of industry say in words and facial expressions that they did not know what had happened or what was to be done about it. They did not understand their own experiment. Then – not till then – did I give up – and turned to see what else there was."[3] "Nobody in the world," he said in another letter, "*proposes* anything basic and real except the Communists."[4]

Something "basic and real" – that was what so many of the young writers were searching for in the early years of the depression. No one was searching more ardently than John Dos Passos. Early in the twenties, as I have said, he had written a bitter attack on war, *Three Soldiers*. In 1925 he published an experimental novel, *Manhattan Transfer*, in which he tried to catch the chaos of a great city. Like many of his contemporaries, he was intensely critical of the quality of American life in the twenties, but, unlike most of them, he asked himself what could be done. In 1926 and 1927

[3] Lincoln Steffens, *Letters of Lincoln Steffens* (New York: Harcourt, Brace & Co., 1938).
[4] *Ibid.*, p. 949.

he interested himself in the case of Sacco and Vanzetti, two Italian anarchists who had been found guilty of murder during the hysteria against foreigners and radicals that followed the First World War. He not only wrote a pamphlet in defense of the two men; he took part in picketing in Boston and was sent to jail for a night.

Almost a decade later, in writing *The Big Money*, the third volume of *USA*, he re-created the emotion he had felt the night Sacco and Vanzetti were executed. One of the devices in *USA* is something called "The Camera Eye," a series of autobiographical reminiscences written in a poetic style. With the Sacco-Vanzetti case, the subjective "Camera Eye" and the objective narrative come together, for several of the characters are also involved in the demonstration. Here is the way Dos Passos sums up:

> they have clubbed us off the streets they are stronger they are rich they hire and fire the politicians the newspaper editors the old judges the small men with reputations the collegepresidents the wardheelers (listen businessmen collegepresidents judges America will not forget her betrayers) they hire the men with guns the uniforms the policecars the patrolwagons
>
> all right you have won you will kill the brave men our friends tonight
>
> there is nothing left to do we are beaten..............
>
> America our nation has been beaten by strangers who have turned our language inside out who have taken the clean words our fathers spoke and made them slimy and foul
>
> their hired men sit on the judge's bench they sit back with their feet on the tables under the dome of the State House they are ignorant of our beliefs they have the dollars the guns the armed forces the powerplants
>
> they have built the electricchair and hired the executioner to throw the switch
>
> all right we are two nations.........................

they have won why are they scared to be seen on the streets? on the streets you see only the downcast faces of the beaten the streets belong to the beaten nation

all the way to the cemetery where the bodies of the immigrants are to be burned we line the curbs in the drizzling rain we crowd the wet sidewalks elbow to elbow silent pale looking with scared eyes at the coffins.

we stand defeated America.[5]

It was not surprising that Dos Passos was one of the first of the literary men to see the depression as a major crisis of the capitalist system, and to take the side of the communists. He was never a member of the Communist party; he described himself as a campfollower rather than a joiner. But he defended the rights of communists, and was one of the founders and for several years treasurer of the National Committee for the Defense of Political Prisoners, which was what would now be called a Communist front. As we have seen, he signed the manifesto of the intellectuals for Foster and Ford.

During this period, when he was most concerned with the economic crisis and with the role of the communists, he wrote what is by general consent – of conservative as well as radical critics – his major work, the three novels that are collectively known as *USA*. In these novels he set forth a broadly inclusive account of American life from about 1900 to about 1929. Nobody had previously attempted so large a design, and there has been nothing quite like it since. It is not a conventional novel, for it describes the lives of fifteen or twenty characters and introduces biographies of historical figures, extracts from newspaper stories, and autobiographical reminiscences. As the three volumes appeared, I was moved

[5] John Dos Passos, *The Big Money* (Vol. III of *USA*) (Boston: Houghton Mifflin Co., 1946), pp. 461–464.

and excited by them as I seldom have been by any other literary work, and, although they do not move me in the same way today, I still think highly of them.

Even before he had finished *USA*, Dos Passos was beginning to be disillusioned with the Communist party, and by the end of the thirties his disillusionment was complete. Since then he has moved steadily towards the right, and in recent years has identified himself with the conservative wing of the Republican party. He has continued to write about the American scene, and has attempted several ambitious works since *USA*, but he has never approximated the power of that work. Somehow the militancy of the years in which it was written released great imaginative powers and gave us a work that has an enduring place in American literature. If a decade can be said to have a literary expression, *USA* is the expression of the thirties.

Dos Passos' disillusionment with communism set a pattern that we shall find frequently repeated. The influence of the Communist party on particular writers was in almost every instance short-lived. But this should not lead us to underestimate the impact of the depression itself. The turn towards communism was a hasty impulse, soon regretted, but questions had been raised about the character of American life that could not easily be answered.

Edmund Wilson, in an essay on Ernest Hemingway, has described with rueful eloquence the impact of the communist vision:

> The progress of the Communist faith among our writers since the beginning of the depression has followed a peculiar course. That the aims and beliefs of Marx and Lenin

should have come through to the minds of the intellectuals who had been educated in the bourgeois tradition as great awakeners of conscience, a great light, was quite natural and wholly desirable. But the conception of the dynamic Marxist will, the exaltation of the Marxist religion seized the members of the professional classes like a capricious contagion or hurricane, which shakes one and leaves his neighbor standing, then returns to lay hold of the second after the first has become quiet again. In the moment of seizure, each one of them saw a scroll unrolled from the heavens, on which Marx and Lenin and Stalin, the Bolsheviks of 1917, the Soviets of the Five-Year Plan, and the GPU of the Moscow trials were all a part of the same great purpose. Later the convert, if he were capable of it, would get over his first phase of snow blindness and learn to see real people and conditions, would study the development of Marxism in terms of nations, periods, personalities, instead of logical deductions from abstract propositions or – as in the case of the more naive or dishonest – of simple incantatory slogans. But for many there was at least a moment when the key to all the mysteries of human nature seemed suddenly to have been placed in their hands, when an infallible guide to thought and behavior seemed to have been given them in a few easy formulas.[6]

This passage has the true autobiographical ring. Wilson had early been aware of the seriousness of the depression, and during 1930 and 1931 he published in the *New Republic* a series of articles on what was going on in the United States – later published in book form as *The American Jitters.* At the same time he wrote for the same magazine an "Appeal to Progressives." American liberals, he said, could not very well cooperate with the Communist party as it was then constituted, but they could and must accept the Communist program: "they

[6] Edmund Wilson, "Hemingway," in *The New Republic* (New York: Harcourt, Brace & Co., 1938).

must take Communism away from the Communists, and take it without ambiguities or reservations, asserting emphatically that their ultimate goal is the ownership of the means of production."[7]

Wilson recovered more quickly than most from his attack of snow blindness, and he soon became outspokenly critical of the American Communist party, even though he had signed the Foster-Ford manifesto of 1932. He continued to be interested in the Communist program, and when he visited Russia in 1935, his report was largely favorable. At the same time he was making a careful study of Marxism and the intellectual traditions out of which it had developed. The book that finally resulted from his arduous studies, *To the Finland Station*, published in 1940, is a major contribution to intellectual history.

Thus throughout most of the decade Wilson was concerned in one way or another with the problems the depression had raised, although he did write some purely literary essays. The decade of discontent had made its mark on him, and, though he is not now a radical in any ordinary sense, that mark can still be seen.

James T. Farrell did not have to wait for the depression to teach him about poverty and hardship; he had seen plenty of both in the course of his Chicago boyhood. *Young Lonigan*, published in 1932, was an attempt to show what could happen to a Chicago kid who grew up tough, rather than an attempt to show the need for revolution. But as he continued with the trilogy, Farrell became increasingly aware of the implications of his

[7] Edmund Wilson, *The Shores of Light* (New York: Farrar, Straus and Young, 1952), p. 532.

story. The story of Studs was as truly an American tragedy as was Dreiser's story of Clyde Griffeths. (Dreiser had a great influence on Farrell's style and his whole approach to literature.) Moreover, as the work progressed, Farrell became increasingly interested in communism and supported some communist causes. When he came to the end of the trilogy, he drew a deliberate parallel between the death of Studs and the collapse of the capitalist system, for Studs's father watches a Communist demonstration as his son is dying.

Farrell soon became an outspoken anti-Stalinist, but he remained for many years an advocate of drastic social change, a staunch member of the anti-Stalinist left, and the strength of his convictions can be felt in his later novels.

It is sometimes hard to remember how pervasive social discontent was in the thirties. It affected many of the older writers. Theodore Dreiser, for example, was active in a variety of communist causes, and he wrote a book of left-wing propaganda, *Tragic America.* (He quarreled with the Communist party after that, but he was a member of it when he died in 1945.) Sherwood Anderson was hit hard by communism for a brief time, and his concern showed itself in a book of essays, *Puzzled America*, and in such novels as *Kit Brandon*. Sinclair Lewis was wary about the Communists, but he did write an anti-fascist novel, *It Can't Happen Here*, which Communist critics welcomed. (He also wrote an anti-Communist novel, *The Prodigal Parents.*)

But it was, naturally, the new writers who reacted most sharply to the depression, and in the middle thirties there was a great spate of so-called proletarian novels.

Most of them have long since been forgotten, and deservedly so. Who remembers the names Myra Page, James Steele, Grace Lumpkin, William Rollins, Arnold B. Armstrong, Clara Weatherwax, or Philip Stevenson?

Yet it is a mistake to suppose that the radical fiction of the thirties was all negligible. There was Jack Conroy, whose novel about a poor miner's family, *The Disinherited*, was recently issued in a paperback edition and proved to be not so irrelevant to life in the year 1965 as we should like to believe. There was Robert Cantwell's *Land of Plenty*, which described with skill and authority a strike in the West Coast lumber industry. (Cantwell, I might say in passing, was one of the really gifted writers of the thirties, but when he lost his radical convictions, as he soon did, he lost all sense of direction, and, though he wrote books of various sorts, he never realized his potentialities as a novelist.) There was Josephine Herbst, who wrote a trilogy describing the decline of the middle class—*Pity Is Not Enough*, *The Executioner Waits*, and *Rope of Gold*—three excellent titles and three excellent books. There was Richard Wright, a Communist for a time, though not a pious one; his first and most powerful novel, *Native Son*, dramatized the racial struggle rather than the class struggle, though Wright tried to show that they were one and the same. There was Henry Roth, whose *Call It Sleep*, first published in 1934, has recently been revived; this was, among other things, a true proletarian novel, though its Marxist critics did not recognize it as such.

I run through these names to demonstrate that, although the thirties was a difficult decade for writers, it was not so sterile as is often said. I have limited myself mostly to writers of fiction, but there were also leftists in other literary spheres. Looking at the index of *Proletarian Literature*, a rather absurd anthology published in 1935, of which I was one of the editors, I find among the poets represented, Horace Gregory, Langston Hughes, Muriel Rukeyser, and Genevieve Taggard; among the dramatists, Clifford Odets and John Howard Lawson; among the critics, Malcolm Cowley, Williams Phillips, and Philip Rahv.

Only a few of the writers I have thus far named were members of the Communist party, but most of them followed the party line at least for a time. The question is often asked: What was the effect of the Communist party on the writers and other artists who were either members or fellow-travelers? There is no doubt in my mind now that the influence was harmful. I do not believe that artists can accept the direction of any political organization, and the direction of the Communist party was particularly dangerous because of its dogmatic and dictatorial character. But we must not assume that all the left-wing writers of the thirties bowed to the dictates of Earl Browder or any other party official. Even the few of us who were party members were not so subject to party discipline as we were supposed to be. If the Soviet Union, after decades of dictatorship, could not eliminate the possibility of a Pasternak, a Zoshchenko, or an Abram Tertz, we should not exaggerate the power of the Communist party in the United States, even in the thirties.

But what is far more significant than the allegiance of a few writers to the Communist party is the effect of the depression and the consequent uneasiness and discontent on writers who owed no such allegiance. Take, for instance, the strange case of Thornton Wilder. In the twenties Wilder published two delicate and mildly fantastic novels, *The Cabala* and *The Bridge of San Luis Rey*, the second having a great popular success. When his third novel, *The Woman of Andros*, a book in the same vein, was published, Mike Gold, a leading Communist literary spokesman, wrote in the *New Republic* a violent attack that stirred up considerable controversy. Why, Gold asked, does Wilder write about Rome and Peru and ancient Greece? "Let Mr. Wilder write a book about modern America," he concluded. "We predict it will reveal all his fundamental silliness and sentimentality."

The interesting thing is that Wilder accepted Gold's challenge, and wrote *Heaven's My Destination.* It is not at all the kind of novel Gold would have liked, but one cannot say that it proved its author either silly or sentimental. It is the story of a young man – a salesman of of textbooks – who is doing his best to be a good man in the conditions of modern society and finding it extremely difficult. George Brush is not a heroic figure; on the contrary, he is, by most people's standards, a good deal of a fool. But his mishaps, like those of Don Quixote, tell us a great deal about the society in which he lives. Although Wilder's criticisms were couched very much in his own language, *Heaven's My Destination* does belong to the critical literature of the thirties.

Or there is the equally strange case of F. Scott Fitzgerald, the epitome of the twenties, the handsome young man who made himself both the recorder and the embodiment of the Jazz Age. No one could have seemed more remote from politics than he, and yet he wrote to his cousin in 1934: "Apropos of our conversation it will interest you to know that I have given up politics. For two years I've gone half haywire trying to reconcile my double allegiance to the class I am part of and the Great Change I believe in. . . . I have become disgusted with the party leadership and have only health enough left for my literary work, so I'm on the sidelines." [8] To his daughter, Scottie, he wrote four years later: "I am known as a left-wing sympathizer and would be proud if you were." [9] He also wrote to Scottie, in a letter that cannot be dated: "Sometime when you feel very brave and defiant and haven't been invited to one particular college function, read the terrible chapter in *Das Kapital* on 'The Working Day,' and see if you are ever quite the same." [10]

It may be said that Fitzgerald's radicalism didn't influence his fiction, and it didn't in any overt way. Yet I think we can now see that *Tender Is the Night*, published in 1934, is in part an experiment in social criticism, and it is interesting to learn that at one point he thought of having Dick Diver denounce the whole capitalist system and go to Russia. He didn't do it, and he would have spoiled the novel if he had, but the very fact of his thinking about it is significant and typical of the times.

Thomas Wolfe was never much interested in politics; some people would say that he was never interested in anything but Thomas Wolfe. Yet in his last novel, *You Can't Go Home Again*, published after his death, he left as moving an account as can be found anywhere of the miseries the depression had brought. His autobio-

[8] F. Scott Fitzgerald, *The Letters of F. Scott Fitzgerald*, Andrew Turnbull, ed. (New York: Chas. Scribner's Sons, 1963), p. 417.
[9] *Op. cit.*, p. 37.
[10] *Op. cit.*, p. 102.

graphical hero, George Webber, wandering the streets of Brooklyn, watches with pity and horror the lives of the jobless and the poor in general. And at the end he seems to be moving to some sort of political decision.

Wolfe himself, before his death in 1938, had come to at least one decision. He had loved Germany, as he said, next to the United States, and he had been much esteemed there; but, visiting the country for the last time in the summer of 1936, he could not close his eyes to the persecution of the Jews. The next year he published in the *New Republic* a long short story, "I Have a Thing to Tell You," describing that persecution and exposing it to the world. (The incident, in a different form, was included in *You Can't Go Home Again.*) From that time forth his books were banned in Nazi Germany.

In a famous passage in *A Farewell to Arms* (1929) Ernest Hemingway had announced his disillusionment with the language of politicians and generals: "I was always embarrassed by the words sacred, glorious, and sacrifice and the expression in vain. We had heard them, sometimes standing in the rain, almost out of earshot, so that only the shouted words came through, and had read them, on proclamations that were slapped up by billposters over other proclamations, now for a long time, and I had seen no glory and the sacrifices were like the stockyards at Chicago if nothing was done with the meat except to bury it." [11] Three years later, in *Death in the Afternoon*, he wrote: "Let those who want to save the world [save it] if you can get to see it clear and as a whole." [12]

[11] Ernest Hemingway, *A Farewell to Arms* (New York: Chas. Scribner's Sons, 1949), p. 196.
[12] Hemingway, *Death in the Afternoon* (New York: Chas. Scribner's Sons, 1932).

Yet by 1937, when he wrote *To Have and Have Not*, he was showing that the salvation of the world was not indifferent to him. Not only does the novel take sides with those who have not against those who have; the hero, a rugged individualist of the piratical sort, discovers that no man alone can fight the system.

Hemingway was now (1937) acutely and practically interested in the Spanish Civil War, not only reporting the conflict but raising considerable sums of money for ambulances and medical supplies for the Loyalists. He also wrote a play, *The Fifth Column*, in which he expressed his sympathies in the most forthright and partisan terms. (It was at this point that Edmund Wilson spoke of Hemingway's snow blindness.) A little later, when the war was over, he wrote his most ambitious novel, *For Whom the Bell Tolls*. Although he could now see that the issue was not so black and white as he had at first supposed, his sympathies were still with the Loyalists, and the quotation from John Donne out of which he drew his title was an affirmation of social responsibility: "No man is an island." The problem of the thirties had its international as well as national aspects, and towards the end of the decade the former were more prominent than the latter. *For Whom the Bell Tolls*, presenting the struggle for freedom as a world-wide struggle, is a representative novel of the thirties and one of the enduring achievements of the decade.

There is one more writer of whom I must speak, John Steinbeck. After two or three poetic novels, he published in 1936 one of the best novels ever written about a strike, *In Dubious Battle*. Although one of the characters is a Communist organizer, the novel advocates neither the Communist program nor any other. (So far as I know, Steinbeck has never had any political affiliations.) It does, however, show a warm sympathy for the oppressed.

It is this sympathy that illuminates *The Grapes of Wrath* (1939), which seems to me the best example I know of a depression-bred novel. To begin with, it deals with a group of the obviously underprivileged, the Oakies, the dispossessed farmers of the Dust Bowl, for whom sympathy is easy, and it portrays them in credibly human terms. In the second place, the kind of political action that it advocates is stated in strictly native language, with no suggestion of Marxist or any other sort of dogma. And, finally, the situation it portrays is remediable, and, indeed, it was largely remedied, in part because of the impact of Steinbeck's novel. I am no great admirer of Steinbeck's later career, and I believe that there were at least twenty American writers more deserving than he of the Nobel Prize, but *The Grapes of Wrath* is still a powerful novel, and in its own time it was a master stroke.

There is only one great name of the thirties — I would now say the greatest — that I have not mentioned, William Faulkner. Although there is evidence that he was affected by the depression, he scarcely alluded to it in his fiction. The reason, I think, can be found in Faulkner's close identification with the Mississippi community in which he had grown up. His roots were in an agrarian, not an industrial, civilization, and the collapse of the industrial economy did not much concern him. He was not indifferent to social problems, but it was with the problems of the land and its people, black and white, that he was engaged.

Although Faulkner was largely ignored in the thirties – when, in fact, he wrote most of his best work – his reputation grew greater and greater in the later forties and fifties. This re-evaluation, like the revival of Henry James, was evidence of an about-face in literary judgments. This was not merely because disillusionment with Soviet Russia had made a whole generation suspicious of political causes, though that was a factor in it. The important thing to remember is that, as I said in the beginning, left-wing literature grew out of a tradition that went back to the 1890's. That tradition had, in a manner of speaking, worn itself out, and the young writers, those coming to maturity in the forties and fifties, wanted a new approach.

The typical writer of the past twenty years seldom deals with large political or economic issues. His characters are not figures in business or government or leaders of social revolt. They are almost always offbeat persons: a kid in a carnival, a street preacher in the South, an adventurer in Africa, a storekeeper in Brooklyn. And they are not seen, as a rule, against a broad social background but in some small and isolated area of life. The typical writer does not ask: How can we remedy injustice? What can we do to build a good society? He asks: Who am I? What is the good life? What must I do to be saved?

As a critic, I feel no obligation to choose between the two traditions. Of the memorable novels of the past, some have been concerned with social problems, others with strictly individual problems. *War and Peace* and *The Brothers Karamazov* are both great novels.

But I am glad that the literature of the thirties is being re-examined. As I have said, I believe that the greatest novels of the decade were written by William Faulkner, who was not directly concerned with social problems. But such works as *USA*, *Studs Lonigan*, *The Grapes of Wrath*, *You Can't Go Home Again*, *For Whom the Bell Tolls*, to say nothing of *To the Finland Station*, some of the plays of Clifford Odets, and at least a small body of poetry, are not to be scorned. The great danger of the decade was political dogmatism, to which many lesser writers succumbed but which the greater writers rose above. Its great virtue was strength of feeling, which, in literature, is not a negligible virtue.

For a time, especially in the fifties, when McCarthyism was polluting the atmosphere, clear analysis of the thirties was difficult. But now we—even those of us who were deeply involved in the struggles and controversies of the period—can begin to take a calm look at it. What we find, as I have tried to demonstrate, is that it was an interesting decade and, in literary terms, not an unproductive one.

NORMAN THOMAS

The Thirties in America as a Socialist Recalls Them

Introduction by Murray Edelman

To a political scientist, the central and intriguing fact about the Socialist party in the 1930's is the disparity between the vote it was able to attract and the acceptance of many of its policies. It has often been noticed that the people whose favorite political party wins do not necessarily get the policies they were promised. The American Socialist party in the 1930's suggests the converse: that a party that cannot come close to winning at the polls may nonetheless see some of its most important policies realized. In fact American third parties often make their poorest showing exactly when their policies become popular enough for the major parties to accept. Political science textbooks cite this as their classic role in the American political system. This record also raises

Murray Edelman is a professor in the Political Science Department, University of Illinois.

some interesting questions about the meaning of "the mainstream of American politics," a term that was not used much in the thirties, but which the thirties can help us to understand.

Many, including Socialists, have contended that the two major parties often represent no real choice. But when, as in 1936, they did present what seemed to be a clear choice, there was a very lopsided vote. (It happened again, as you may remember, in 1964.) There is then no possibility of a party outside the mainstream being elected; and if both parties do represent the mainstream, is there a choice? The effect of this situation is to reinforce the idea of a clear policy choice without actually presenting one.

In 1936, the Socialist party, whose vote that year was far below what it had been in 1930 or even in 1932, was closer to the policy mainstream than were the Republicans. I suspect that the Socialists watched with some eagerness as Democrats adopted policies they had long recommended in such fields as tariffs and trade barriers, labor legislation, social legislation, social security, and some areas of the farm policy, such as the Resettlement Administration. The bearing of elections on policy is a complicated issue.

Norman Thomas' contribution to the political life of the 1930's went beyond advocacy of policies in and between election campaigns. He was a tireless worker for causes that the Democrats would not, or politically could not expouse, as well as some they did: votes for Negro sharecroppers, freedom in Jersey City and so on. I suspect almost everyone in this audience over forty-five remembers hearing him on the radio and in shabby halls in the thirties, and remembers the buoyant and compelling voice, that in a sense was also copied by the New Deal.

Norman Thomas was born in 1884. He received his A.B. from Princeton in 1905 and in 1932 Princeton conferred a Doctorate of Literature on him. In that connection it is interesting to remember that in 1912 he was a registered Republican. He has done a great deal of editorial work. For a time he was editor of *The Nation.* He writes a column for the *Denver Post* and is the author of many books. He ran twice for mayor of New York City, once for governor of New York State, and he was a candidate for President of the United States in every election from 1928 to 1948.

Unlike some of the participants in this series, his stature did not reach its peak in the 1930's. His moral authority has grown; and his has been a career that prepares a man for analysis and serious re-examination of his work. He is going to do some of that re-examination for us as he discusses the Socialist movement in the 1930's.

FOR THE PURPOSE OF THIS LECTURE, I shall regard the thirties under discussion as beginning with the stock market crash on Wall Street late in 1929 and ending with our entry into the Second World War in 1941. It is impossible to examine any period as if it had existed in a vacuum. Therefore, it will be necessary to say a few words about the earlier years of the century and to remind you that my appraisal of the thirties will be unconsciously, if not consciously, influenced by more recent events to which the thirties were a prelude.

Walter Lord, a popular historian, has written a book, *The Good Years*, about the years from the beginning of the twentieth century to the First World War. I have always thought the title well chosen. They were the good years of my life for various reasons—among them, a sense of optimism and hope about progress, with a capital "P." But there was plenty wrong with those years, more than I realized at the time. One reason for the optimism was the general conviction that there would be no more big wars, certainly not those involving the

United States. Along with it went a notion which I never shared, at least fully, that imperialism represented by our policy in the Philippines could be benevolent and an expression of manifest destiny.

In 1910, Norman Angell published his famous book, *The Great Illusion*, which demonstrated that in the world as it then was, war meant loss to everyone. The book was universally applauded by the high and mighty of the earth. Then came the First World War and the kind of optimism which had gone along with Wilson's first election and the Bull Moose brand of Progressivism; the steadily increasing vote for Eugene V. Debs disappeared, never to return again. The notion that we fought the war to make the world safe for democracy was never valid, although a great many Americans were hypnotized into believing it. It is a fair observation to say that we would never have fought the war if we could have traded with both sides as prosperously as we had traded with the Allies.

The war under the liberal Woodrow Wilson, who had previously made racial segregation the rule in federal office buildings, worked havoc with civil liberty. Such idealism as there was in the notion of the League of Nations met political defeat. We had first the era of the Palmer Raids while Wilson was still President. Then the Harding administration began and with it came a very sharp and cynical reaction on the subject of the war and its legacies.

Prohibition was in its way a moral victory succeeded by a wholesale violation of the law. Its curious role as a political issue was seen in the campaign of 1928, and its defeat and repeal came comparatively early in the Roosevelt administration.

Under Coolidge there was a hectic stock market prosperity. Employment was pretty good, but successful organization of the workers made slow progress. For the first time workers began to be personally interested in the stock market. I remember hearing a ticket seller on the Chicago "El" talking to another worker rather early one morning on the platform; they were discussing stocks much as one might have discussed the numbers racket.

In this atmosphere, Herbert Hoover, much respected for his relief work and for his supposed knowledge of economics, won the first presidential campaign in which I was a candidate. The issues were prohibition and Protestantism *vs.* Catholicism. In my own travels I discovered that Al Smith, Democratic candidate, was unpopular in many parts of the country, not just because he was a Catholic and a "wet," but because "he talked like a New Yorker." I heard a group on a street corner in Ohio rejecting him because he said "rahdio." When Hoover was inaugurated, the unhealthy boom was still on. A chicken in every pot and two cars in every garage was an American ambition.

In 1929 I was a candidate for mayor of New York City, I ran against the dapper and popular Jimmy Walker and the able congressman, Fiorello LaGuardia, who at times flirted with socialism. Under the conditions of campaigning as they then prevailed, candidates often crossed each other's trails at schoolhouses and other regional meeting places. At one such meeting, I taunted LaGuardia, with whom I was on very friendly personal terms, for his lack of program. He and I were both making an issue of Tammany corruption. I, however, as a Socialist candidate, had what was for its date a fairly specific program covering a great many matters which are now commonplace in the current mayoralty campaign. As we left the meeting LaGuardia said, in a querulous voice, "Norman, you know I only had the Republican endorsement. How could I have a program?"

The local elections of 1929 occurred shortly after the stock market crash but before the spirit of the twenties could be dissipated. The difference between the campaign of 1929 and the campaign which LaGuardia won in 1933 was itself indicative of the profound changes which the depression brought. The descent from a false prosperity into the depths of the Great Depression of the thirties was sudden and catastrophic. American politicians and the capitalist system generally had no injection of Keynesianism to save them or to ameliorate the poverty which suddenly fell upon them. The general wage and salary average was scandalously low in prosperous 1929. The average per capita income derived from wages and salaries for all groups was approximately $1,475. In 1932 it had fallen to $1,119. Unemployment increased tremendously. By the summer of 1934, after things had improved a little, there were some ten million unemployed and the number was then rising, not falling. The New Deal did not rapidly restore employment, although it fairly rapidly provided some form of relief by providing special work or otherwise.

The very rich did not escape. In 1929, the number of men and women who confessed to incomes in excess of one million dollars a year was 513. In 1932, it had fallen to 20. This in spite of the fact that in the first full year of depression, while wages declined by 8 per cent, dividends and interest better than maintained themselves.

By 1932, a very considerable part of the American

population was living in what were called Hoover-villes — extraordinary shelters made of junk. They were a feature of the landscape of 1932. For some reason I recall with special vividness the Hooverville on the levee at St. Louis and the one by the bank of the Canadian River in Oklahoma City.

Farmers suffered relatively as much as workers, except that more of them had homes of their own and land on which to grow food for themselves. Nevertheless, it was a curious fact that by 1932 violent opposition to the law and to conditions was more conspicuous among farmers. The most miserable of the farmers, sharecroppers in the South and day laborers on the land, were — and still are — so badly rewarded for their toil that even depression could hardly make things worse. It was ironic for them that the advent of the first measures for improving the agricultural situation, plowing under corn, cotton, etc., actually worsened conditions and were more responsible for the trek to California described in Steinbeck's *Grapes of Wrath* than were the factors to which Mr. Steinbeck had attributed the cause.

It is, as I look back upon it, amazing that the workers were so comparatively quiet. There were strikes of desperation, all of which were lost. The autocratic John L. Lewis, head of the relatively powerful coal miners' union, generally refused to sanction these local strikes. In many districts he was hated by his men. It was only after passage of the National Recovery Act (NRA) that he became an outstanding figure in building the CIO on the basis of industrial unionism.

The chance for citizens to speak out as voters came with the presidential campaign of 1932, when the Great

Depression was three years old. The situation has produced many would-be saviors of the lost economy. The most popular were Huey Long, governor, senator, and "boss" of Louisiana, and Father Coughlin, Roman Catholic priest of Detroit, who had an immense radio audience until he was silenced by his church superiors during the Roosevelt administration. But talk of a new antidepression party came to nothing. The field was left to the Republicans, Democrats (who had recovered from their smashing defeat of 1928), and the weak but very vocal Socialist and Communist parties.

In spite of the public resentment at a broken-down system, neither the Republican nor the Democratic parties offered any specific, well-thought-out programs for recovery. The platforms of the two major parties were virtually interchangeable. The Republicans renominated Hoover, who had complained that his office was a kind of hairshirt but who said that he badly wanted to keep on trying. Franklin D. Roosevelt, governor of New York, won the Democratic nomination. He gathered the beginnings of what was later called his "brain trust" about him, but waged a conventional campaign. He even promised to balance the budget and reduce taxes. He called for no more direct government action in the field of economics than that which Hoover had been trying out. Indeed, the distinguished lawyer, John W. Davis Democratic candidate for President in 1924, told *New York Times* readers that he was still a Democrat, partly because none of his predecessors had carried the country so near to socialism as had Herbert Hoover.

As the Socialist candidate for President, I went all over the country without ever hearing or reading more than conventional party praise of Mr. Roosevelt, except that praising his courage in conquering his physical handicap. Roosevelt was elected because he was *not* Mr. Hoover. In later campaigns he was elected because he *was* Mr. Roosevelt.

Feeling against Mr. Hoover was very strong and was expressed in many leaflets for which no party assumed responsibility. One of the most popular was a parody of the Twenty-third Psalm which began, "Hoover is my shepherd; I shall do nothing but want." I sometimes told audiences that it was unfair to put so much blame on Hoover. No one man was big enough to cause so big a depression. Its cause was the system. My only surprise is that the vote against him was not even greater.

The popular election left us with a lame-duck Congress and a defeated chief executive for almost four months until the inaugural date of March 4, 1933. Things went from bad to worse. Mr. Roosevelt refused any cooperation in efforts Mr. Hoover was making. (Before you blame Roosevelt too much, you must remember that he was in a stronger position to act, politically and psychologically, after March 4th. However, you may also want to remember that it was a New York state–chartered bank that precipitated the bank crash and that he, as governor of New York, had done nothing to avert it, in spite of warnings.)

Between the popular election and the inauguration, I continued to do much speaking, by no means wholly in the New York City area. Never before or since have I heard so much open and bitter cynicism about democracy and the American system as in these months. Things were getting steadily worse; Roosevelt seemed to be doing nothing and offering nothing. The cynicism and near despair would in time have played into the hands of organized communism, or into the hands of organized socialism.

The change made by Roosevelt's inauguration and his first hundred days in office was extraordinary. He brought back hope and confidence. The people responded to his own ebullience and his pragmatic program. He was no theoretician; he was a good Machiavellian. He once told me what indeed he also said publicly – that he was saving capitalism and he resented the criticism of those he was saving. He was a Machiavellian in action without the more immoral connotations of the word. He had a high sense of the politically expedient. He left to his wife any effective championship of racial justice. Nevetheless, between 1933 and the validation of the Wagner Labor Act by the Supreme Court in 1937, he securely laid the foundations of our present welfare state.

He did it by making ideas and proposals formerly called "socialist" and voiced in our platforms beginning with Debs in 1900 seem to be immediate demands. Only in the Tennessee Valley Authority (really Senator George Norris' brainchild) and in rural electrification did he seriously challenge and abridge along socialist lines the capitalist system of private ownership and operations for profit. He did accept governmental responsibility for relieving poverty and unemployment and he favored labor organization, which was made more easily possible and almost necessary under his Blue Eagle, NRA program. An enthusiastic Italian journalist told me that he would go back and tell Mussolini that he had seen Mussolini's corporate state over here and that it worked.

As a matter of fact it did not as time went on. Its only

virtue was the boost it gave to labor organization. It turned out to be Roosevelt's luck when the Supreme Court of the "nine old men" declared the NRA unconstitutional, because it gave Roosevelt a justified issue against the Court's assertion of power and it ridded him of an uncomfortable problem.

The recklessness with which the Court of the nine old men knocked out social legislation passed by Congress held a very serious threat to any economic reform by federal political action. It led Roosevelt to advance his dubiously regarded Court-packing plan. Previously socialists had persuaded Congressman Fiorello LaGuardia to introduce a constitutional amendment, mainly the work of Morris Hillquit, which would give the Court power to protect civil liberties, including what we now call civil rights, but not the right to balk Congress in the necessarily shifting field of property rights.

The whole matter was settled when the Court, somewhat changed in personnel, was led through the statesmanship of Chief Justice Charles Evans Hughes to approve the Wagner Labor Act. Approval of the Wagner Act marked a turning point in the Court's approach to a flexible understanding of the rights of Congress to legislate for the social good in a changing economy.

Soon after that decision, during the middle of Roosevelt's second term, the New Deal lost much of its imaginative punch. The welfare state was functioning fairly well but it took the Second World War to reduce unemployment from its shameful heights. Roosevelt was later to say the New Deal became "Win the War," and I sometimes think that Roosevelt, half-way at least, welcomed the change from domestic to foreign policy as our most important concern.

Despite the vociferous outcries from business and other conservatives, the basic ideas of the pragmatic New Deal were rather easily and fully accepted. In 1936 James P. Warburg wrote a pamphlet arguing that any platform Mr. Roosevelt had carried out was mine and the Socialists', rather than his. (In fact, he had accepted only our immediate demands, but not our essential socialism.) The Republicans ordered thousands of Mr. Warburg's book but were thrown into confusion when he announced his intention to vote for Mr. Roosevelt.

By 1940, Wendell Willkie (Ickes' barefoot boy from Wall Street) was close to Roosevelt in domestic and foreign policy. And by that time the overriding issue was the Nazi menace and America's attitude toward World War II. It was that war, rather than the New Deal, which really ended the economic depression and the unemployment associated with it.

Before we examine that issue, we must take a closer look at those movements which had sprung up out of the war, allegedly fought and won to make the world safe for democracy at the end of the century's second decade. Their development, their resemblances and differences, their search for power, dominated the thirties. The thirties also saw the beginning of the awakening of colonial peoples and the emergence of Gandhi as a world figure in stark contrast to Hitler and Stalin.

I can best examine these movements and their impact on the United States from the standpoint of a democratic socialist. Socialism from its earliest days has had many varieties and most of them appeared in America about as soon as they appeared in Europe. We had religious communes, Owenite colonies, radical labor organizations (of which the IWW was most important), and avowed socialist parties in the nineteenth and early twentieth centuries. We also had various types of anarchists. The IWW with its mistrust of political action could be classified as its own sort of syndicalist. On this issue it split from the American Socialist party in 1912.

The American Socialist party, to which I belong, was formed out of a union of socialist groups in the Midwest and secessionists from the dogmatic, quasi-syndicalist Socialist Labor party led by Daniel De Leon. Our party began as a coalition in 1900 which nominated the much loved and hated Eugene Victor Debs for President. On the eve of World War I it had a dues-paying membership of around one hundred thousand and had elected many local officials and one congressman. It suffered severely from the oppressive tactics of the Wilson administration in the war. I never thought this persecution a primary cause of the party's postwar loss of strength. In an Atlanta prison, Debs got around one million votes, and New York state in 1918 had elected five Socialist assemblymen. The great trouble was the Communist split.

At the beginning of the thirties there was in the United States a pretty strong communist movement which had grown out of the split with socialists a decade earlier. There was the main Communist party, loyal in every respect to Russian leadership, and a dwindling party, led by Jay Lovestone, who had been deposed from leadership of the American party by Stalin. (Mr. Lovestone now writes George Meany's foreign policy and claims no socialist allegiance of any sort.)

It may be hard for the present generation to understand the enormous appeal of the Russian Revolution to

American radicals and to many liberals in terms of sympathy. The Russian Revolution meant the overthrow of the most despotic autocracy in Europe. It was the one sure gain of the First World War. Its chief enemies, the capitalists and imperialists, were our chief enemies. It spoke and acted—so it claimed—in the name of the working class whose triumph was bound to mean the ultimate triumph of justice and true democracy even if it had incidental evils, largely the fault of the enemies who opposed it. As late as the beginning of the thirties we had little or no accurate picture of what the Bolshevik government was doing or what its effects were. Communication was difficult. Both sides deliberately lied to win their cause and even the more honest reports were colored with ideological sympathies. It is probable that our Socialist party would have voted to join Lenin's new Communist International party had he not tried to dictate the rejection of our own leaders.

By the beginning of the thirties a little more was known about the real facts in Russia; the line between democracy and totalitarianism had been more clearly seen, and the resentment of the shifting, anything-to-win Communist tactics was more deeply felt. But for socialists, the rising fascism and the old hard-line capitalism were our enemies. We were disturbed by the old problem of when does reform become the enemy of revolution?

Communist tactics, always dictated from Russia, were bewildering. In 1924 Communists had been rejected from the coalition which backed La Follette for President on a frankly reformist rather than revolutionary platform. In 1928, when I first ran for President on the Socialist ticket, and in 1932 the avowed Communist interest was to create a Soviet America in the Bolshevik image. The change to united front tactics came around the beginning of 1935. I was urged in 1936 by Earl Browder, then the Communist leader, to join in creating a labor party which would be more or less sympathetic to Roosevelt. Failing that, I was urged to campaign in 1936 in terms very sympathetic to a Roosevelt victory.

The Communists – the best of them – were devoted people, able in organizing labor and the unemployed. One often wanted to work with them. But their tactics were completely unscrupulous. The great Lenin had taught them that that is ethical which advances the interests of the Communist party. This was, I thought, a monstrous doctrine. But you must remember that it is only slightly more dogmatic than the Mississippian's view of ethics in terms of white supremacy, or than every man's belief that winning his nation's war justifies almost any inhumanity or, when it is useful, any deceit.

Even during the united front period, in the thirties, the Communist manual said that the Soviet Union was the only fatherland of the workers, and continued to support a program of subversion within united fronts and labor unions. The great Trotsky himself, from his exile in Mexico after his expulsion by Stalin, advised his American followers how to get into the Socialist party and how to capture it. Their attempts failed. They got in but they were expelled. Later, one of their leaders taunted me with having believed their original assurances. Meanwhile I had been denied a visa to Russia in the united front period because I had been on the John Dewey Committee for Justice to Trotsky. Under some pressure the Russian foreign office reversed itself and gave my wife and me visas for a visit, during which we were very closely watched.

The history of varying Communist tactics included a violent attempt to break up our great Socialist mass meeting in Madison Square Garden to support the Austrian Socialist workers when their homes were fired on by Dollfuss in Vienna. In my own case the Communists sometimes courted me and sometimes slandered me. In World War II, when they were 212° Fahrenheit patriots because of our necessary alliance with Stalin, they tried to break up an all-too-small meeting which I had organized in behalf of the outrageously dispossessed Japanese and Japanese-Americans on the West Coast. In the 1944 campaign they tried to get the government to prevent me from giving speeches to incite a mob to break up a meeting in Seattle. Their effort, not very intense, failed. (I was then supporting the war but criticizing Roosevelt's approach to peace by unconditional surrender and unnecessary concessions to Stalin.)

Socialists consistently supported civil liberties against anti-Communist legislation and police action. We did not believe in fighting Communism by emulation. We did not think the Communists guilty of acts of violence or subversion against the government, even in those unions in which they had considerable power. But they lost most of this power after the infamous Hitler-Stalin Pact and never to any great degree recovered after Hitler's violation of it. Before the Hitler pact, they had been stoutly pro-labor and antifascist, as of course, had we Socialists.

Before World War II, there had been much profascist and pro-Nazi sympathy in America but no really large-scale and successful organization of an American fascist movement. (Huey Long and Father Coughlin could not fairly be called fascist although their followings might have developed into more definite movements.) There were attempts at fascist movements, one of which was the Khaki Shirts of America, which I am proud to say I had some part in breaking up. (For this kind of service, especially to Italian-American antifascists, I rather recently received the Italian Order of Solidarity, which I accepted in a kind of representative capacity for our socialist and labor comrades in that good cause.)

In this situation it was probably inevitable that there should be vehement controversy in the Socialist party over how revolutionary it should be and how we should respond to the varying tactics of the Communist party. This went on all through the thirties until the convention of 1936 and was a source of weakness to us.

In 1936 our right wing, mostly New Yorkers, broke off because of their fear that we might form some sort of united front with communists. Ironically our convention then adopted a no–united-front policy and we went ahead with our own ticket. In New York state the secessionists, some of them good socialists and valuable workers, decided to join the new pro-Roosevelt American Labor party, in which they for some years cooperated with communists as we had never done. Later they split off to form the Liberal party, which still exists in New York state. The American Labor party died.

During all this unpleasant period of intraparty struggle, I kept an informal poll of comrades who left us for Roosevelt. They were almost equally divided between the right and the left. After 1932 we could get no prominent labor men on our ticket. Comrades who had difficulty working together and who differed vociferously on socialist ideological lines had no difficulty working together for Roosevelt, the "opportunist" whom they had all more or less sharply criticized. (I want, however, to testify to the self-sacrificing devotion with which party comrades supported our ticket and myself in 1932 and in my New York campaigns.)

Our main loss of voting strength in the thirties was not due to the Communists, who never acquired strength at the polls, but to Roosevelt and the general conditions which prevented any third party in America from growing like an oak from an acorn. The way we elect a President, the control of election machinery by forty-eight different states, now fifty, the enormous expense of campaigning, and the willingness of one or both of the major parties to take over popular issues, account for the situation.

The failure of the La Follette coalition to produce a real farmer labor party cost us Socialists dearly. The year 1928 saw a tolerable rebuilding job and 1932 brought us wide hearing and support. But the latter was less apparent at the polls than we had hoped, partly because quite often our votes weren't counted. (Paul Anderson of the *St. Louis Post-Dispatch* reckoned that Jim Maurer and I got some two and one-half million votes.) But the real trouble was that even in that year there were so many voters who agreed with the little old lady at a San Francisco rally who said: "Mr. Thomas, I agreed with all you said, but I'm not going to vote for you. Not this year. We've got to get that man [Hoover]."

Our political influence was not to be measured solely by our vote. In the thirties Socialists were active in organizing the unemployed, in organizing the workers, and helping in the rise of the CIO. H. L. Mitchell, then a Socialist party man in Arkansas, called my attention to the plight of the sharecroppers under the Roosevelt-Wallace program for curtailing production of food and textiles in a hungry world. We can claim to have been pioneers in tackling rural poverty. We also led in free speech fights like that against Mayor Hague in Jersey City.

But with the Franco rebellion in democratic Spain, the growth of Italian fascism and German Nazism, and the power of Communist totalitarianism, foreign policy and fear of a new world war were dominant considerations. It took the war economy really to end the depression. In 1944 I heard men rather shamefacedly hope that war would continue so they could pay off old mortgages or keep jobs.

In my old age looking back on my life, I can admit various mistakes, but I regret no major decisions, except possibly my opposition to American entry into World War II. In saying that, I am admitting a terrible opinion of mankind which condemned us to no alternative but war to triumph over Nazism. I had been a religious pacifist in World War I, and, on socialist grounds, an opponent to our entry. This I never regretted. As time went on, to my sorrow I felt obliged to modify my religious pacifism. I kept my hatred of war but believed support of the Spanish Loyalists a lesser evil than their submission to Franco, backed as he was by Mussolini and Hitler. Socialists did what we could to help. We did not believe that it was the business of the United States to intervene by force, but we opposed Roosevelt's embargo on arms and we aided young men to go to help the Loyalists until bitter experience with Stalin's tactics made it impossible. (There was one case where his secret police kidnapped and presumably killed a volunteer in Spain whose only crime was to be a son of Abramovitch, the Russian Menshevik who had become an American citizen.)

Hitler ended that war by a practice blitzkrieg from which the Franco-British allies learned nothing. My hatred of war, my belief in general European cynicism, and my sense of war's futility were increased. But I was no isolationist. I shared the socialist disappointment at the League of Nations. But both my party and I, without much enthusiasm, supported our entry into the League on easily attainable terms. It was Roosevelt in 1932 who made an end of any talk of joining. We were not isolationists, but I came home in 1937 resolved to fight any entry into war. I helped to form a Keep America Out of War Committee and two or three times later spoke on America First platforms, always explaining that I was not an isolationist except from war and that I was a member of my own committee. Generally the party followed my line although the secessionists of 1936 and some other leading socialists did not. By and large neither we nor the secessionists, who had set up their own socialist groups, gained or lost by this policy.

Many persons forget that Roosevelt, however anxious he was to help the Allies, in his 1940 campaign promised the fathers and mothers of America that he would not send their sons into war. As a matter of fact we did not go as crusaders into the war. Japan made the sneak attack at Pearl Harbor and Hitler declared war on us. The result was the first war in American history to which there was no political opposition but only conscientious objection to all war. With the latter, under the circumstances, I could not agree, and I gave critical support to the war. We immediately dissolved the Keep America Out of War Congress and formed the rather poorly named Post War World Council which was concerned with a just and reasonable peace and an international organization to succeed the defunct League of Nations.

All this lies out of my examination of the thirties. In retrospect, I think the war was the only available way to deal with Nazism although I am equally persuaded that it might have been averted had governments at the Versailles Conference done some of the things socialists had advocated. We learned so little from World War I. Many Americans in the twenties and thirties learned to regret our entry and adopted a too-simple belief that any war would be caused by rival imperialists and "merchants of death," to quote the title of a fairly popular antiwar book.

Whatever my doubts about my opposition to American entry into World War II, I have no doubts about the excellence of the Socialist party's 1944 platform and our approach to peace. The decade which had begun with a country caught in a false prosperity ended with America caught in war. It had, however, seen the definite adoption of a welfare state that might be changed and improved but could not be abandoned. To that much progress and to the preservation of some degree of democracy against fascism or communism socialists made some contribution. Our service is not ended though our tactics and some of our program may be modified. And if I live to Moses' age, 120, I shall not look back with any doubt on the Socialist party's present foreign policy, including our opposition to military intervention in the Dominican Republic and South Vietnam.

A. J. MUSTE

My Experience in the Labor and Radical Struggles of the Thirties

Introduction by Rudolph Vecoli

For half a century Mr. Muste has been a radical activist in the cause of peace and social justice. It was he who pioneered in the use of nonviolent resistance as a technique of social action.

Mr. Muste was born in the Netherlands, coming to America in steerage at age six. He grew up in the Dutch community of Grand Rapids, Michigan. Excelling in academic studies, oratory, and basketball, young Muste attended Hope College from which he received an A.B. and an A.M. He pursued his training for the ministry at the Graduate Theological Seminary of the Reformed Church in America and

Rudolph Vecoli is an associate professor in the History Department, University of Illinois.

at the Union Theological Seminary. In 1909, he was ordained a minister of the Reformed Church. Despite extreme pressures, Muste held steadfast to his pacifist convictions during the First World War; in consequence he was forced to resign from his church in Newtonville, Massachusetts.

Always sensitive to injustice and exploitation, Muste took up the cause of the Lawrence, Massachusetts, textile workers during the strike of 1919. His effective leadership in that strike led to his election as general secretary of the Amalgamated Textile Workers, a short-lived industrial union. From 1921 to 1933, Muste was director of Brookwood Labor College, an institution dedicated to the training of militant, progressive labor leaders. Becoming a Trotskyist Marxist-Leninist, Muste bent his efforts in the thirties to the creation of a revolutionary labor movement. Through the Conference for Progressive Labor Action and the American Workers party (the Musteites), he exerted a limited but significant influence on the political currents of the depression decade. During the thirties, Muste was active in numerous strikes and organizing campaigns, such as the Toledo Auto-Lite strike, the General Motors strike, and the Goodyear Tire and Rubber strike.

A religious experience in the Parisian Church at St. Sulpice in 1936 brought Muste back to Christianity, but did not affect his radical stance on issues of peace and social justice. In 1940 he became executive secretary of the Fellowship of Reconciliation in the United States, a post which he held until 1953 when he became secretary emeritus. In recent years Muste has concentrated on the development of a "radical, politically relevant, nonviolence movement" to oppose the drift toward a nuclear holocaust. As chairman of the Committee for Nonviolent Action, member of the executive committee of the War Resisters' League, and participant in Omaha Action, the Voyage of the Golden Rule, and other peace activities, Muste has remained true to his principle of teaching by example as well as by word. Of late he has been a vocal critic of United States policy in Viet Nam, which he regards as "illegal, disastrous, and immoral." An editor of *Liberation* magazine, Muste is also the author of *Nonviolence in an Aggressive World* (1938) and *Not by Might* (1947). He is the subject of a biography, *Peace Agitator* (1963), by Nat Hentoff.

ON FRIDAY, FEBRUARY 4, 1966, NEWSPAPERS throughout the country carried the news that "a Presidential blue-ribbon National Commission on Technology, Automation and Economic Progress" had issued a report stating that the federal government should guarantee every American family a minimum annual income of perhaps $3000 per year. Other recommendations in the report were that the federal government should provide for free education through the junior college level, that blue-collar workers be paid annual salaries instead of hourly rates, and that half a million jobs should be created, at a first-year cost of two billion dollars, for the "hard core jobless" in hospitals, schools, police departments, and "other useful community enterprises."

The Commission was indeed a "blue-ribbon" one, though it would hardly have been so regarded in the United States of three decades ago, which is the subject of this paper. The two leading members of the Commission are Thomas J. Watson, Jr., board chairman of the IBM Corporation and Walter Reuther, president of the United Automobile Workers Union. The Commission included four executives of corporate industry in addition to Mr. Watson and two labor union executives in addition to Mr. Reuther. The other members were labor arbitrators and college professors, all members of what might be called "the Liberal Establishment."

The headlines announcing this event struck me as I was in the midst of trying to recall the social and political events and atmosphere of the thirties and left me gasping at the contrast between then and now. The nation in the 1930's had just begun to emerge from a depression that appeared to have shaken the very foundations of its economy. My three sisters and their families were typical of thousands upon thousands who had lost or all but lost the homes they had acquired by twenty years of toil and arduous saving. The unemployed were still organizing and picketing to get enough relief to fend off hunger, and to make it possible for children to attend public schools clothed in something a little better than rags. The workers in the mass industries were engaged, as the decade of the thirties wore on, in an epochal and bloody struggle for the right to organize. If any group had come forward with proposals remotely resembling those of the Watson-Reuther Commission, its members would have been denounced, not in polite or even printable language, as utopian dreamers and Bolsheviks.

Even now, let me note in passing, Arthur Krock in the *New York Times* of February 6, 1966, commented that if the recommendations of the Presidential Commission were to become "the state of the Union without wrecking it . . . the American form of government would have been supplanted by a Socialist system in which public power is totally federalized." Mr. Krock closed his column, however, with a remarkable tribute to a man who had been battling in the thirties for a program considerably more moderate. After expressing the opinion that Congress may be coming to the point of disapproving the more radical of the Great Society legislative proposals, he concluded, "But if any of them became law, it is to be hoped Norman Thomas will still be around to administer them. He is the only citizen in sight who is both learned in the philosophy of socialism and who knows the responsible limits to enforcing it in the American society." It is superfluous to remark that such an observation by a conservative columnist on the *New York Times* is another revealing instance of the psychological distance between now and then.

Let me turn now to my experience in the labor and radical movements of the thirties. The first section will center around Brookwood Labor College, a resident institution with an extension program, located on an estate near Katonah, New York, in suburban northern Westchester County. It was founded in September of 1921 and ceased to exist in 1937. My own connection with it was terminated in the spring of 1933.

My direct contact with the labor struggle had begun early in 1919 in a strike of 30,000 textile workers in Lawrence, Massachusetts, shortly after the World War I armistice. With two other young Protestant ministers who had lost their pulpits during the war because of their pacifism, I had gone to Lawrence when it became evident that another mass strike would break out in that city which had been the scene of a dramatic strike under IWW leadership in 1912.

Perhaps now I should state the inner attitude and the conviction which took a young pacifist clergyman, quite inexperienced in such matters, into a turbulent strike situation, led him to accept after a few days what amounted to leadership of that strike, and brought him lifelong involvement in one way or another in social and political struggles. So far as my own reading goes, it is best expressed in the writings of Martin Buber. What Buber calls "the religious-normative principle" manifests itself as an essentially historical one. There is an indissoluble relation between the superhistorical and history; "the superhistorical molds the historical but does not replace it." At another point in his book *At the Turning*,[1] Buber refers to those who find in God an escape from nature and history but contends that this is the very opposite of the relations of the God of Israel toward creation and history. "He has placed man in the center of reality in order that he should face up to it."[2] This leads to a perpetual, often anguished, and seemingly futile effort which Buber sets forth in the sentence: "True, it is a difficult, a tremendously difficult undertaking to drive the plowshare of the normative principle into the hard sod of political fact; but the right to lift a historical moment into the light of superhistory can be bought no cheaper."[3]

During the four months' strike in Lawrence, a national organization of textile workers was formed. Substantially aided by Sidney Hillman's Amalgamated Clothing Workers of America, it was named Amalgamated Textile Workers of America (A.T.W. of A.). (Hillman was the Sidney of Franklin D. Roosevelt's "Clear it with Sidney" instruction to New Deal politicians in the thirties.) I became National Secretary of the A.T.W. of A.

The early twenties were not favorable to the establishment of unions in the textile industry. The administration of a labor union was hardly a natural occupation

[1] Martin Buber, *At The Turning: Three Addresses on Judaism* (New York: Farrar, Straus and Young, 1952).
[2] *Ibid.*
[3] *Ibid.*

for me. One episode of that period merits mention. It was during my term as national secretary that Moscow set up the Red International of Labor Unions as a rival to the non-Communist International. The A.T.W. of A. was one of the unions invited to become a charter member. Many of the young textile workers on our executive board were impressed by the invitation and were also favorably disposed to the Russian Revolution in that early heroic period. My argument, that a union which had as yet few stable local affiliates in the United States had no business representing itself as a national body which could honestly take part in establishing a world organization, won out, and the A.T.W. of A. did not send a delegate to that Moscow gathering.

In the summer of 1921 a number of leading progressive trade unionists such as James Maurer, head of the Pennsylvania Federation of Labor; John Fitzpatrick, the fighting head of the Chicago Federation of Labor; and Fannie Cohn of the International Ladies Garment Workers Union, together with some leading educators, including John Dewey, were interested in developing a labor education movement in this country that would be modeled after the movement in Great Britain. One of their objectives was the establishment of a resident college for active workers in unions. The estate in Westchester County was made available to them and in September, 1921, Brookwood Labor College opened its doors to its first class. At the urging of the founding group, I resigned my position with the A.T.W. of A. and became educational director of the school.

The college, which did not bestow degrees or give grades or certificates of any kind, did not make any pretense of being neutral. It was identified with the labor movement and in a broad sense with the struggles of the workers. Its labor directors and faculty members were progressives or radicals. No political lines were drawn in admitting students so that typically the student body included conservative trade unionists as well as Communist party members. On the other hand, the school was not under the control of any party. It was influenced by Marxist thought but it was not Marxist. The faculty members were chosen for their competence as scholars and teachers. In their classrooms and in their life outside the classroom and school they had complete freedom. The unifying central concern was to contribute to the development of a trade union, political, and cultural movement adapted to the American scene and to contribute to the achievement of a democratic society.

Brookwood had the support of a number of the more progressive labor unions and the respect of many figures of the academic and intellectual community. By the same token it was from the outset suspect to the hierarchy of the American Federation of Labor in the Coolidge-Hoover era. In August, 1928, at the annual convention of the American Federation of Labor (A.F. of L.) in New Orleans, all affiliates of the Federation were urged to withdraw support from the college and to warn their members from coming under its dangerous radical influence. The condemnation was based on a secret report by Vice-President Matthew Woll to the executive council of the Federation. The trade union members of the Brookwood College Board pleaded in vain with their trade union brethren to grant them the democratic right to see the report on the basis of which they and the institution were condemned. Their plea was denied. It was rumored in reliable circles that an important item in the list of charges was that May Day was observed at Brookwood and that at a recent May Day celebration the portrait of Samuel Gompers, deceased revered leader of the A.F. of L., was hung side by side with that of Eugene Debs and Nikolai Lenin. The offense, it was implied, would not have been so serious if Gompers' portrait had been left out. Another feature of the 1928 A.F. of L. convention was the condemnation of John Dewey as a pernicious and subversive influence in American society.

Brookwood weathered that crisis. None of the trade union members of the board of directors resigned. Students kept on coming. Graduates, many of whom had proved their devotion and competence in the unions to which they had returned, remained loyal. Despite the depression, the school managed to remain financially solvent.

The essential integrity of the course it has pursued is presumably attested by the fact that about the same time the Communist Young Workers League (Y.W.L.) warned *its* members to stay away from Brookwood. It proclaimed: "Brookwood is no more Communist than the Executive Board of the A.F. of L. itself. . . . The YWL will continue its struggle aganst Brookwood and its ideology and will make every effort to destroy whatever influence it may have among the working youth." The *Daily Worker* commented that Brookwood's fate at the hands of the executive council is "one more demonstration that those who stand neither with the right nor the left get the bricks from both extremes."

Brookwood encountered a truly serious crisis in 1933 and it may be said that it arose largely out of the effort to "stand neither with the right nor with the left" to which certain participants, including myself, in the social and political struggles of the thirties were committed.

The Communist party, having weathered its struggles with the Trotskyist left and the Lovestoneite right, and having expelled them both, settled down to its involvement in the big organizing campaigns which followed New Deal legislation establishing the right to organize and bargain collectively. Largely because of the efforts its members and leaders threw into the strikes and organizing campaigns of the early and middle thirties, Communists gained a foothold in many unions and control in a considerable number. Many working-class elements and many intellectuals were drawn into the party or its front organizations.

The Socialist party, which had exercised a great influence in the garment trades unions and in the mining sections of the country, lost much of its appeal when many of its "immediate demands" were incorporated into Roosevelt's New Deal legislation. It was afflicted by internal conflicts. Most important, the leaders of the garment trades unions, who had experienced bitter struggle for union control with the Communists in the twenties, now found relief from unemployment and poverty for their members in the gradual emergence of the economy from the depths of depression. Concurrently, they were drawn into the Roosevelt orbit and the Roosevelt-Democratic coalition. They carried their members with them and were thus also delivered once and for all from internecine battles with Communists. At the same time, the Socialist party lost its foothold and its source of moral and financial support in these unions.

In these circumstances, people who had been connected in some way with Brookwood, who had been radicalized by the depression but could not go along with the Communist party nor follow confidently in Roosevelt's train, felt a need for an instrumentality that would enable them to operate in the mass struggles of the new period.

That instrument was in its initial form the Conference for Progressive Labor Action (C.P.L.A.). It actually came into being in the twenties and originally included trade unionists and a number of Socialist party members and leaders. The C.P.L.A. sought to combat gangsterism and corruption in the labor unions. It condemned the A.F. of L., largely composed of craft unions, for its failure to tackle seriously the job of organizing the workers in the basic industries into industrial unions. It urged political action, preferably in the form of a labor party, fashioned on the lines of the British Labor party.

The C.P.L.A. provided leadership and financial support to strikes, especially in the textile and mining industries where conditions were distressing and A.F. of L. leadership indifferent. In a number of states or sections of states, it organized the unemployed into militant Unemployed Leagues which served several purposes, such as providing an outlet for local workers' leadership, giving a sense of dignity to the unemployed who were no longer passively submitting to their lot, actually ameliorating their condition somewhat, and contributing to the channeling of dissent which, among other things, led to the election of Roosevelt in 1932.

The Communist party had its own organizations known as Unemployed Councils. They were more numerous than the Leagues because the Communists had larger forces at their command than did the C.P.L.A. But in no place where the Leagues were set up were the Councils able to get a foothold.

Let me now comment on the crisis which overtook Brookwood in 1933. In the beginning the C.P.L.A. had been largely an arm of Brookwood, its faculty members were members or sympathizers. The strikes in which the C.P.L.A. was involved tended to be in industries from which Brookwood's students came. In turn, some of the ablest students came out of these struggles and enriched the life of the school. Graduates in other industries were virtually all keenly aware of the low estate of unionism, and regarded activity in the C.P.L.A. as a natural result of Brookwood training.

As the political developments created the vacuum which I sketched a moment ago, and when the advent of the Roosevelt era opened up possibilities for activity in the field, some of the Brookwood staff, including myself, were drawn to devote more attention to these field activities under C.P.L.A. sponsorship. We thought that Brookwood should emphasize its extensive activities to link education directly with organizing and strike activities. We were prepared to consider selling the Brookwood property and to use the money to establish the headquarters of the school in some industrial center. That the school was experiencing financial difficulties of course introduced tension into the controversy. A very important factor in the situation, as I look back, I think the basic one, was a political factor. Some of us moved to the left. We took on a deeply critical attitude toward the Roosevelt regime. We attempted to form a non-communist left adapted to American conditions, and we refused to support World War II. Others were drawn into the Roosevelt orbit, took posts in the C.I.O. unions, and eventually supported the war.

Trade union members of the board of directors had the majority vote in a corporation in which faculty members, graduates, and students also had votes. The trade union members (perhaps with some reluctance) voted against the policy which I was advocating, as did the majority of the faculty. The majority of students and graduates were on my side. The result was that in the spring of 1933, I retired as Brookwood's director. The break was a trying one for all who were caught in it because in a real sense we had been a "community" and not an educational "institution." The school had hard sledding following the break. It is ironical that this was in no small sense due to the fact that as the big organizing campaigns in automobiles, steel, aluminum, etc., got under way, every worker who was worth his salt was needed in the struggle and could not be spared to go to a labor college for a year. At the same time, the new or nascent unions had to step up their educational programs on the spot. I do not cite this as conclusive evidence that our approach would have worked, since that would have depended on our relationship to the leaders of the new unions and on our attitude toward the trend which they subsequently followed.

The result was that I now devoted full time to the C.P.L.A. and to its successor organizations for several years. The first episode that I should note here is an experience with the Communist party in the trade union field. The Communist party had undertaken organizing independent unions in a number of industries when the New Deal legislation improved the prospects for unionization. I had always been strongly opposed to trade union policy to organize unions as rivals to the A.F. of L. or independent unions because I considered it divisive. I had also consistently opposed the policy of using unions as instruments to be manipulated for party purposes. The early New Deal days, however, seemed to present a new situation and consequently new possibilities. In important basic industries, there were no unions. Many of us were convinced that the A.F. of L. hierarchy would make no effective or even serious effort to organize industrial unions in these key industries. The events, as witness the opposition the C.I.O. organizing efforts encountered and its eventual, though temporary, separation from the A.F. of L., bore out our analysis in this respect.

Under the circumstances, it appeared that a vacuum existed or was threatened and that there might be an opening for an effort to set up industrial unions, independent of the old trade union structure and radically oriented. The C.P.L.A. people were also firmly convinced that to be successful the new industrial unions had to be free from Communist party control and manipulation. Communist party trade union specialists approached the C.P.L.A. people with the idea of combining forces and initiating a number of organizing campaigns in basic industries along C.P.L.A. lines.

The Communist party already had small nuclei of "industrial unions" in several industries, the leaders of which were those who would naturally participate in a conference without joining forces with us. We laid down the condition, however, that in no case would any of these Communist party units be regarded as the nucleus of the new unions, because this would have meant that our forces would simply be drawn into a Communist party organizing campaign. The new union was in each case to be built from the ground up and not to be under party control. A conference was held in Cleveland. After the usual preliminaries the delegates were divided by industries – steel, glass, automobile, etc. – and proceeded to discuss procedures for their respective industries. These industry sessions had been under way for less than an hour before it was reported that the Communists were arguing that the Communist "industrial union" be the nucleus for the organizing campaign and that their Trade Union Unity League be the central body.

I immediately informed the Communist leaders that we refused to continue on this basis and that unless it was immediately changed we would leave. They would not budge. They acquiesced in calling a plenary session, in which I explained the circumstances of our withdrawal. No attempt to reply was made. Before I left the building, some of the Communist trade union leaders offered me the leadership of *their* Trade Union Unity League. I have no idea why they did, to this day.

Again, I observe that it is ironical that the Communist party gained its eventual very extensive influence in the unions by abandoning its essentially sectarian approach and by sending its forces into the C.I.O. organizing campaigns. In some cases they were used by astute leaders like John L. Lewis and Philip Murray (United Mine Workers), who were basically anticommunist and always themselves in control. In other cases, Communists did exercise control and probably on the whole did a good job in strictly union matters, only to have their control challenged and in most cases broken in the post–World War II McCarthy era.

The C.P.L.A. continued to play an active and to some extent leading role in the strikes which marked the beginning of the huge and eventually successful efforts to organize the basic industries and establish the C.I.O. Notable among them was the Toledo Auto-Lite strike in 1933. At a later date we were closely involved in the rubber strikes in Akron, Ohio, where the sit-in tactic was introduced.

After the Auto-Lite strike I went to southern and central Illinois to report to our followers there on the Auto-Lite experience. One morning with two young miners, I drove to a struck metal plant on the outskirts of Belleville, Illinois. The plant was closed and only two strikers were present. The five of us sat down on the grass. A police car was parked across the street. Three policemen walked over and asked us for identification. They looked at the red C.P.L.A. membership cards which the three of us carried. When at a preliminary hearing one of the policemen was asked by a Civil Liberties Union lawyer from St. Louis why he had arrested me, he answered: "I thought that any preacher who was traveling like that so far from his home must be up to some mischief." Perhaps he had something there. At any rate, I was indicted under the Illinois "treason statute," a relic of the A. Mitchell Palmer days, for conspiring to overthrow the State of Illinois by force and violence. After I had spent some days in jail, friends from the Illinois Miners succeeded in raising the $20,000 bail. After about a year the charge was dropped.

THE AMERICAN WORKERS PARTY

It was almost inevitable that the C.P.L.A. activists and adherents, not finding the Socialist or Communist parties satisfactory and being profoundly skeptical as to where the New Deal was going, should attempt to form their own political party. There were well-known intellectuals, such as Sidney Hook, James Burnham, and Max Eastman, who supported the idea. Accordingly, the C.P.L.A. toward the end of 1933 was transformed into the American Workers party (A.W.P.). It was intended to be, as someone quite correctly stated, "a democratically organized revolutionary party" seeking to build on the American revolutionary tradition and to function on an American and not Russian or other base.

However, the A.W.P. had hardly gotten under way when the Trotskyists, who had abandoned the idea of fighting their way back into the Communist party and were functioning as the Communist League of America, approached us and proposed that merger be discussed. The A.W.P. people, who had started as labor activists and who had proved competent in that field, had been politicalized in the course of their experiences and were trying to build a political (party) home. The Trotskyists had, of course, come out of the Communist party but had developed a strong desire to play a part in mass organization. Some of their leaders had led teamster strikes in Minneapolis, which involved virtually all the unions and seemed to have revolutionary possibilities.

The merger seemed natural or at least well worth trying to the overwhelming majority of the leaders and members in both groups and it was consummated after prolonged discussions in 1935. The Communists were disturbed and infuriated. The *Daily Worker* warned the Musteites against "the trap of counter-revolutionary Trotskyism"; it warned Trotskyists against "unity with Muste, the champion of bourgeois nationalism." The new party was named Workers Party, U.S.A.

We were now members of the so-called Fourth International which Trotsky had founded after being exiled from Russia and after he was convinced that the Third (Stalinist) International could not be redeemed. As I have been thinking back on those days, the chorus of a satiric song written some years later keeps running through my mind. It goes: "There's the First International, the Second International, the Third International, [louder] the Fourth International, [then still louder] but we are the members of the Last International and there won't be any more." The authors may have magically divined the current Moscow-Peking split.

The collaboration from which much had been expected soon became a troubled one. It revolved around a tactic devised by Trotsky and which was known in Fourth International circles as the "French Turn." Trotsky had a strong following in France. The Socialist party in that country under the leadership of Leon Blum was an impressive force. France was threatened also by fascist elements and the threat of an attack by Nazi Germany hung over it. The Communist party was seeking to build its own front against war and fascism. Under the circumstances, for reasons that are easily discernible, Trotsky decided that his followers should join the Socialist party as a faction which would bore from within. He ordered them to do so, and I say "ordered" deliberately because I became convinced that though in many respects very different from Stalin, Trotsky was no less a dictator in his own party than Stalin was in his.

I did not have a clear judgment then as to whether under the conditions in France in the mid-thirties — so few short years from the upheaval of 1939 — the "French Turn" was morally justifiable and politically advisable.

I do not have a clear judgment on that now. But I was quite sure that the application of the "French Turn" to the United States, i.e., entry of the newly formed W.P.U.S.A. into the (Norman Thomas) Socialist party, would not be morally justifiable or politically sound. We told this to the Communist League leaders before the merger and were assured that there was no thought whatever of applying the tactic here.

Nevertheless, only a few months after the W.P.U.S.A. had been formed, one of the former Communist League leaders introduced at a meeting of our politbureau (we had now adopted this verbiage) a resolution that the desirability of entering into the Socialist party be explored. At the time there were radical younger elements in the Socialist party who regarded the party as reformist and wanted it to become revolutionary, and who therefore welcomed the idea of the merger. Discussions, to which I was not invited, took place between them and the old-time Trotskyists in the W.P.U.S.A.

The Musteites and I fought the proposal. Apart from other considerations, I was convinced that entry into the Socialist party would only weaken that organization and would divert the energies of the Workers party from mass action and party building. The idea, of course, was to enter the Socialist party in order to radicalize it. This would be achieved by drawing the revolutionaries out of it after a time, and channeling them into the Fourth International. Although nominally the W.P.U.S.A. went out of existence when all of us were accepted into membership in the Socialist party, actually the politbureau of the Workers party met as usual the Monday after we had ceased to exist and functioned as a manipulative faction within the Socialist party.

My deductions were in this case correct. In less than two years the Trotskyists were expelled from the Socialist party for divisive activities. James Cannon, the leading American Trotskyist, told a reporter some years later that he remembers telling Trotsky about the weakened condition in which his forces had left the Socialist party and that "Comrade Trotsky said that that alone would have justified our entry into the organization even if we hadn't gained a single member." To me this statement is one of many proofs that in his later years the brilliant Trotsky almost completely lost touch with reality. In any case, the American Trotskyists did not grow and soon were themselves torn by factional struggles.

Here I must bring into this account of my experiences in the social and political struggles of the thirties a person with whom I was closely associated in those years and who must be included in any account of the period. This is Louis F. Budenz. I met him first in the early twenties. He had come to New York out of a circle of militant liberals in St. Louis, whence Roger N. Baldwin, principal founder and for many years leader of the American Civil Liberties Union, had also come. He established and kept going for a number of years a monthly publication called *Labor Age* which was to all intents and purposes, though not formally, an organ of the C.P.L.A.

Budenz was a phenomenally effective organizer of strikes and demonstrations. Though one would not have guessed it from his appearance, he had no rival in those days as a speaker who could sway masses of workers and bring them out of the mill and mine to the picket line. From the beginning he was a key figure in the C.P.L.A. and in the A.W.P. when that came into being. When later

I looked back on the discussions about merger with the Communist League, I realized clearly what I had all along suspected – that Budenz lacked enthusiasm for that move. He did not, however, openly dissent from the step when it was finally taken and the A.W.P. was enrolled in W.P.U.S.A.

His break with it was under circumstances as dramatic as one can conceive. I have already spoken of my opposition to the proposal to infiltrate the Socialist party. During the weeks when a hot internal discussion raged over the issue, Budenz was laid up with a painful siege of sinus trouble. I visited him from time to time. It was clear that he also opposed the "French Turn" but he gave me no hint whatever of the move he contemplated and no doubt had already secretly carried out. On the morning of the day when the crucial debate over the issue was to take place in the New York local of the W.P.U.S.A. – a meeting which would be decisive since that local contained a very large percentage of the total national membership – his secret was revealed. Not having read the news on the way to the meeting, I was greeted on entering the hall with the news that Budenz, Arnold Johnson, and a few less important members of the A.W.P. had joined the Communist party. The startling development naturally somewhat weakened my position in the debate. Some of the hard-core Trotskyists may even have suspected that most of the Musteites and even Muste himself were already secret members of the Communist party. That was not, however, the case, and the suspicion, if it existed, was not brought out in the debate.

There was another dramatic development that morning, however. There were a number of former members of the Communist League who had become members of the Muste caucus because they opposed the application of the "French Turn" to the United States. That group received a cable from Trotsky himself, then in exile in Norway. It was a statement advising them to support entry into the Socialist party. It was couched in terms which constituted an "order" in my opinion. It certainly immensely strengthened the Cannon-Shachtman caucus in the ensuing debate. The outcome of that debate was in favor of the Socialist party entry, but not by a large majority.

As for Budenz, his entry into the Communist party at that juncture was understandable to me. He had always cherished an emotional attachment to the Soviet Union, perhaps one should say to the Soviet people, though he was critical of many aspects of Stalinism. He had become convinced that Trotskyist policy was bound to weaken the Soviet Union seriously in a period when the rise of Hitler in Germany threatened that country. The Communist party, under the leadership of Earl Browder, was entering a period when its propaganda emphasized the American revolutionary tradition, as Budenz had always done. It also turned to an emphasis on union organizing and began to exercise formidable influence under the Roosevelt regime, two policies that Budenz had always advocated. The period of the U.S.-Soviet alliance in the war against Nazi Germany must have been one of profound satisfaction to him as editor of the *Daily Worker* and a figure of some importance in the Communist party high command.

In my view it is also understandable that when the break between the U.S. and the U.S.S.R. developed after World War II, when Earl Browder was expelled from the Communist party and when the party line hardened and its role in the unions was weakened, Budenz' enthusiasm for the party should have cooled. That he should have returned to the Roman Catholic Church is also understandable to me and in a sense to be expected after the inner conflict he must have endured at times as a leader of the Communist party in the United States when the world Communist movement was still under Stalin's domination. He had been under the religious instruction of Fulton J. Sheen and had been a convert to Catholicism for some time before he publicly severed his connection with the Communists and was publicly received back into the Church.

What is not understandable to me, except on grounds which subjects his integrity to question, is that Budenz should have become a crusader for anti-Communism, a witness for the infamous House Un-American Activities Committee, and a factor of some importance in the McCarthyite scourge. Members of the Roman Catholic hierarchy in the United States may have had a good deal to do with this turn on Budenz' part. When the news of Budenz' return to the Church broke and it was hinted that he might become an anti-Communist crusader, I wrote him a personal letter in the hope that it might lead to a renewal of friendship and a dialogue in which I might dissuade him from such a course. There was no reply from him and we have never met since that time.

I must now speak of the turn in my own life and activity following the decision of the W.P.U.S.A. to enter the Socialist party. At the outset I submitted to the majority decision and nominally became a Socialist party member. The controversy had been an exhausting one and in the spring of 1936 friends of many different persuasions got together a purse to send my wife and me to Europe for a vacation. It was somewhat contradictory but natural enough under the circumstances that our first stop should have been Norway for a week's conference with Leon Trotsky who was there in exile. In Norway a good many Labor party members were sympathetic to the Fourth International and the government was a civilized one. Trotsky and his wife were the guests, in a small town near Oslo, of a Labor party editor who had spent some years in the U.S. with the I.W.W. in the twenties and whom I had known in those days.

During the week when I had numerous discussions with Trotsky, I was greatly impressed with him as a human being and with his intellectual versatility and brilliance. He tried very hard to persuade me to stay in the party. At the end of our talks, somewhat to my surprise, he said to me in effect that an American version of the "French Turn" was not the right tactic, but it had been done and I should not let it drive me out of the party to which I had too much to give. James P. Cannon, foremost leader of American Trotskyists, reported many years later that when I broke with them, "Trotsky specifically cautioned me in a personal letter to keep the dispute within fraternal limits and to be careful not to say or do anything that would strike at Muste's prestige."

My next stop on that trip was Paris for a secret meeting of the leaders of the Fourth International from many countries. A considerable number of them were as strongly opposed as I to the application of the "French Turn" in their respective countries, but as I have mentioned before, Trotsky dominated the party and the "line" was adhered to.

Then the "vacation" began which took us to Switzerland and then back to Paris. There I began the process of reflection, which led to my decision to break with the Trotskyist caucus in the Socialist party and to let my pseudomembership in the Socialist party lapse. I made my decision public in September, 1936. I had come to reject the dogmatic Marxism-Leninism for which, as I came to see it, the Trotskyists stood. I was convinced that the concentration on political maneuvering which was bound to follow the entry into the Socialist party would virtually eliminate our effectiveness in the mass struggles which were taking place in the basic industries. The way in which the entry into the Socialist party was carried out and its underlying purpose were in my mind a violation of working-class ethics which I could not stomach. To continue to operate in that atmosphere was impossible for me.

Other factors, however, were involved which have a close relevance to the crisis in which America finds itself in the world of 1966, so vastly different in many respects from the world of 1936. To these matters I devote the closing section of this survey.

What happened to me in Paris that summer was in one aspect a psychological experience which can be characterized as a religious conversion or reconversion. It led me to return to the Fellowship of Reconciliation, a religious pacifist body, and to a new commitment to nonviolence both as a way of life and as a strategy, a truly revolutionary strategy, for social change. Closely related to these developments was my reading of what was happening to Europe and the world as I looked at it from a broader perspective than that of intensive involvement in labor and political activity in the United States.

Nineteen thirty-six was the year when Hitler's new air force engaged in its ominous and dramatic maneuvers over the German countryside and cities. It was the year of the Spanish Civil War, which was the forerunner and training ground for the great war to come, as today's Viet Nam may conceivably yet prove to be for a greater war to come. It was the year when the British Labor party abandoned its policy of opposition to British rearmament.

What I saw, heard, and sensed in Europe during those weeks left me absolutely convinced that World War II was coming, that it had to all intents and purposes begun, and that nothing would stop it and that the United States would be even more totally involved than it had been in World War I. This conviction forced me to reconsider virtually all aspects of my own life and activity and of political and social developments generally.

Specifically, I had to evaluate what was happening with the unfolding of the New Deal and other domestic developments in the light of the conviction that we were headed for war, that Roosevelt would lead us into it (I am not hinting at a dark conspiracy on his part or a personal love of war or anything of that sort), and that however the domestic crisis might be met in an America still in some sense isolated from world events, the overriding fact of our lives was that a world upheaval was brewing which would engulf the nation and American society. It was this coming event which constituted the real problem, the solution to which the future of America and of mankind depended upon.

The domestic problem which had been posed by the depression was "solved," partly by the step-up in arms production which was a part of the preparation for participation in the war which did break out in Europe in 1939. America did become involved, openly and fully after the attack on Pearl Harbor.

A strong case for participation in that war could be made and was. The nation backed the war in a sense that does not remotely resemble the backing of the current sorry conflict in Southeast Asia. It should be observed that Roosevelt's domestic policies, which favored unionism and did ameliorate economic conditions, had a good deal to do with the fact that there was so little resistance in labor and other circles to this foreign policy. Also, of course, the war meant jobs as well as casualties.

However, when one reflects on the present state of the world, on the devastation wrought in Europe and Japan, and the situation in Santo Domingo and Viet Nam, it is certainly clear that the problem of world relations in the nuclear age has not been solved, that as is commonly remarked, human survival may now be at stake. In any case, the existence of affluence in the United States and the fact that in the economic field such proposals can be made today that would have been stigmatized as "Bolshevik" in 1936, does not at all mean that the basic problems of American society are being solved. In some sense what is happening domestically aggravates the problem. The problem of poverty, for example, is most acutely one of the poor in Asia, Africa, and Latin America, not in the U.S. Those poor are getting poorer while America grows richer. The labor movement in the United States today is solid and unreflective in its attitudes toward the Viet Nam war and its support of the Johnson policies; again an important factor is that the administration's domestic policies are regarded on the whole as favorable to labor. There are jobs to be had in transporting supplies as well as soldiers to Viet Nam. But the Great Society, if there is to be one, will be a world phenomenon, not an American one. It will depend ultimately on how the United States resolves its relationships to the rest of the world, and whether the menace of war in the atomic age is dissipated.

HAL DRAPER

The Student Movement of the Thirties: A Political History

Introduction by Joseph Gusfield

The American student has been volatile and inconstant in his political activity. He has had periods of relative inaction and periods of sudden and explosive activity. In 1770, for instance, Harvard students, in an effort to force the dismissal of a hated tutor, engaged in the most terroristic act one could perform. They threatened to resign en masse and transfer to Yale. In the pre–Civil War era, students helped operate the Underground Railway that ferried slaves to the North and freedom. On campuses, riots and demonstrations were held in response to campus conditions and curriculum as well as to national political events.

Joseph Gusfield is a professor in the Sociology Department, University of Illinois.

In contrast to the periods immediately preceding and following the thirties, the depression decade was also an era marked by heightened student involvement in domestic and international problems. And to paraphrase the Bible, "After many a silent autumn, the voice of the student is heard once more in the land." While Hal Draper will limit his remarks to the period of the thirties, he has also had first-hand experience with the contemporary student movement that began on the Berkeley campus of the University of California a few years ago. Mr. Draper is unique in having been involved with students' movements spanning two generations and representing distinct types.

In an introduction to Hal Draper's recent book, *Berkeley: The New Student Revolt*, Mario Savio, the student leader of the "Free Speech Movement" on the Berkeley campus, described the author as follows: "Hal Draper is one of the few 'over thirty' who were familiar with the events of the struggles from the very beginning and who understood well enough to take the students seriously. He has always been ready with encouragement, but has consistently refrained from giving inappropriate and unsolicited 'vintage 1930' advice. This is far from common with our 'fathers.'"

Hal Draper was born in New York City. He attended New York University and Brooklyn College and graduated from the latter in 1934. In 1932 he joined the Socialist Student League for Industrial Democracy as it was getting under way; then the Young People's Socialist League. He became active as a leader in both organizations. In 1934, he was one of the founders of the American Youth Congress and a member of its first national committee. In that same year, he helped organize the largest anti-war strike in the country. In 1935, when the American Student Union was founded, he became a member of its first national committee and remained on the committee until 1937.

After 1937, he spent many years as a socialist organizer and writer, particularly for the Independent Socialist League in

New York, Boston, Philadelphia, and Los Angeles. For a number of years, he was editor of its magazine, *The New International*, and of its weekly newspaper, *Labor Action*.

At present, in addition to being a part-time staff member of the University of California library at Berkeley, he is one of the editors and founders of the quarterly magazine *New Politics* and chairman of the Independent Socialist Committee, an unaffiliated educational project.

MOST OF THE REFERENCES ONE hears to the student movement of the thirties, and most published references too, are quite wrong in one basic respect: they speak as if "the thirties" represented a single, homogeneous period for the student movement. But the biggest single fact about the history of this movement is that it went through a sweeping change in spirit, methods, and politics, which changed its face completely in mid-course. The present sketch will concern itself mainly with that transformation.[1]

1

This movement was newborn in 1931; it was not the continuator of a previously existing one. During the

[1] There is no published material on this, but a sound treatment can be found in the unpublished Ph.D. dissertation by George P. Rawick, *The New Deal and Youth* (University of Wisconsin, 1957). This is without doubt the only attempt at an outline history of the movement that is worth reading; it has the added advantage of including also the closely related story of the American Youth Congress as well as of the New Deal youth agencies. Also still worth reading is the 1935 book by the National Student League leader James Wechsler, *Revolt on the Campus* (New York: Covici-Friede, 1935), even though it deals with only the first period of the movement and of course is written entirely from the then NSL viewpoint. For this first period, it is especially good for great detail on the issues and battles of the student movement, about which I have put very little into this essay. I have leaned heavily on both Rawick and Wechsler's accounts for the factual framework.

twenties there had been a small movement around a magazine called *The New Student*, but it had never created much of a stir. The "Lost Generation" reflected in F. Scott Fitzgerald's novels was (as he wrote in one of them) "a new generation . . . grown up to find all gods dead, all wars fought, all faiths in men shaken." The rebels too reflected the malaise of the society they rebelled against, as is so often true. *The New Student* thought that what was needed was a revolt in "manners and morals"; youth had to save the broken-down old world; some kind of change was necessary, something had to be done; "spiritually, this is an age of ruin and nausea." By 1923–24 there were a number of campus battles; but by 1924–25 "normalcy" and prosperity were returning, and *The New Student*'s interests turned amorphously toward moral indignation with such phenomena as the growing "gigantism" of the universities, the evils of commercialized education, and the "quality of life." With increasing depoliticalization, the movement decayed into Menckenism, particularly enamored of Mencken's derision of bourgeois society from an elitist standpoint – one which was as contemptuous of the mass of people as it was of the "booboisie." By 1927 the magazine was confessing that "Where we used to dream of new faith and new communities developing out of colleges and flowering through a thankful country, now the main hope is that students will be less bored by lecturing. . . ." And by 1928 it was through. For the bulk of students, what reigned supreme were football, fraternities, and sex.

Then in 1929 the bottom fell out. It seemed as if the bottom had fallen out of the whole economic system. For there was no natural famine, no devastating war, no plague: it was as if the social machine simply broke inside and had ground to a halt. There was something referred to as "overproduction," which meant that too much wealth had been produced; and since there was too much wealth, millions were unemployed, factories were shut down, and breadlines grew. Apple sellers became a street sight; vaudeville entertainers sang "Buddy, Can You Spare a Dime?" The bodies of financial magnates rained down from upper stories of Wall Street executive suites; and other tycoons, like Charles M. Schwab, were convinced that the Social Revolution was just around the corner.

The social group hardest hit by the depression was the youth. In 1930, the census figure for unemployed of all ages was 3,187,647, and about one-fourth of these were in the fifteen to twenty-four age range. (According to other estimates, over one-third.) As of January, 1935, there were 2,876,800 youths between sixteen and twenty-four years of age who were on relief; and this was about 14 per cent of the total for this age group. In 1938, one out of every five youths in the labor market was either totally unemployed or on work relief (not counting those working only part-time). This was the youth problem of the thirties: "unemployment for between 20 percent and 30 percent of all youth; scanty education for the great bulk of youth from families in the lower-income brackets; and an extreme intensification of all problems for Negro youth. Youth made up more than its share of the one-third of a nation ill-clothed, ill-housed and ill-fed."[2]

For this "Locked-Out Generation," the prospects of the student youth were correspondingly dim.

[2] Rawick, *The New Deal and Youth.*

In 1935 one college president told a student assembly that the 150,000 students with degrees were emerging into a world which did not want them. A Columbia University official said: "the social order is unable to absorb those who are annually graduated from our colleges and professional schools." (This was often true even for the highest-ranking men.) Another well-known educational institution, the U.S. Army, was getting a stream of college graduates at its Whitehall Street recruiting station in New York, and the New York *Post* explained that the attraction was "grub, prosaic grub." In 1934, the year I was graduated, it was estimated that one-third of the previous graduating class had been able to obtain no employment at all, and that another third had gotten jobs for which they had no interest, talent, or training. One college journal addressed an editorial to the graduating class headed "Into the Wasteland." There was an "Ode to Higher Education," of which one variation went like this:

> I sing in praise of college,
> Of M.A.'s and Ph.D.'s,
> But in pursuit of knowledge
> We are starving by degrees.

All this meant two other things, too: first, it was increasingly difficult to work one's way through college; and second, retrenchment in educational budgets reduced the opportunity for other students to go to college. A *Harper's* article of 1935 said: "In many respects, the post-1929 college graduate is the American tragedy. He is all dressed up with no place to go. . . ."

A whole section of the American middle class was being declassed; and the student movement was in part a result of this declassment.

2

The student movement that arose was initiated and launched by two radical youth groups, working separately: the Young Socialists and the Young Communists. This fact determined its whole history. Let us begin with the Socialist wing.

There had been a socialist student organization in existence since 1905, when Jack London, Upton Sinclair, and others formed the Intercollegiate Socialist Society. The I.S.S. later became the League for Industrial Democracy, an adult organization which maintained an intercollegiate department. But after the First World War, the college section of the LID was small and amounted to very little during the 1920's. It was only with the onset of the depression that it began to grow. Two years after the stock market crash the LID's annual student conference, held at Union Theological Seminary on the theme of "Guiding the Revolution," assembled 200 representatives from 44 colleges. In the presidential election of 1932 the Socialist candidate was Norman Thomas, whose campaign drew in a considerable number of students (including myself) and helped to build the LID's student organization.

By December, 1932 the college arm of the LID – at this point called the Intercollegiate Student Council – was chafing at being merely a department of an adult organization; and it was also facing competition from the Communists, as we shall see. Reorganization as an autonomous Student League for Industrial Democracy (SLID) gave it its own structure and a more independent life, but it never achieved independence in one respect: financially. The adult LID continued to pay its officers, whom it had originally appointed, and these remained, as before, Joseph P. Lash and Molly Yard. Lash, a graduate of The City College of New York in his early twenties, remained on as executive secretary of the SLID, and later of the American Student Union, right through the thirties, with Miss Yard as his first lieutenant. Both were members of the Socialist party. Lash also became editor of the SLID's new magazine, first called *Revolt* but quickly toned down to the *Student Outlook*.

It must be explained that the SLID was an amalgam of two fairly different kinds of socialist students: the "Yipsels" and the "LID types." The "LID types" were essentially liberal-social-democratic in their approach to politics, and sometimes not very political at all; they often tended to be colored by pacifist, Christian socialist views, and not infrequently were more liberalistic than socialistic. A young man at Swarthmore named Clark Kerr could fit into the SLID chapter there. In their own way, both Lash and Molly Yard were "LID types."

Numerically more important than the "LID types" were the student members of the Young Peoples Socialist League (YPSL—youth section of the Socialist party), commonly called "Yipsels." In the larger cities, where there were substantial young socialist groups, the Yipsels tended to dominate the SLID chapters, especially in New York City. (As student director of the New York organization of YPSL for several years, I was largely concerned with mobilizing Yipsels to help build the SLID chapters in the city.)

It is important to understand that, by and large, at this time, the young Socialists constituted the left wing of a Socialist party which was itself rapidly going left throughout this period. The YPSL leaders, and an overwhelming majority of its membership, considered themselves to be revolutionary socialists, and, far from being influenced by the Communists in this regard, were utterly contemptuous of them, especially when the communist movement swung right after 1935. The Socialist party also swung sharply left in the thirties, though not enough to please the Yipsels. By 1935, as a result of the increased radicalization of its members and the influx of younger, more militant recruits, the party's extreme right wing (the "Old Guard") walked out. Later that year, the party accepted into its ranks the whole Trotskyist group (Workers party, with its youth group, the Spartacus Youth League, many of whom were already active in the student movement). Both the loss and the gain served to shift the balance of politics in the party even more to the left – until the latter part of 1937 when another split took place in the party along left-right lines, with the large majority of the youth organization going along with the left wing.

As long as the tone of the student movement remained militant, i.e., up to 1935, the tension implicit in the coexistence of these two socialist strains within the SLID occasioned little or no hostility. Besides, particular SLID chapters were usually either Yipsel-dominated or else "LID-ish," and went their own ways in practice, as "hards" and "softs," respectively. It was only with the rightward turn in 1935 that a clash developed.

3

The other source of the student movement came from the Communist students, and eventuated in the building of the National Student League. This part of the story is usually represented under the heading, "Communist Conspiracy Decides to Capture the College Campuses," etc. What actually happened is a good deal more interesting and more complex. Both for this initiatory period and for the later turns and changing course of the student movement's leadership, it is indispensable to understand the coeval turns of the Communist party line, which constitute the background. On the basis of this background, the story of what happened to the student movement is as clear as crystal; without this background, it is an insoluble mystery.

In 1929 the Communist International had launched all of its parties into what it baptized the "Third Period," a period of wildly ultra-left and ultra-sectarian policies. The motivation came from the needs of the Russian regime. Having already liquidated the Trotskyist left opposition, the Stalin dictatorship now consolidated itself by turning against the Bukharin "right wing," and was driving hard toward the crystallization of the new Stalinist society in the image of the new ruling class. Internally, the turn toward mass bureaucratic collectivization of the land meant the adoption of terroristic policies toward the peasantry, and a rigidification of the party leadership's autocracy in all aspects of life.

Translated into terms of the satellite parties' tactics, the result was lunatic-fringe politics. (Maoist China, together with its faithful Maoist parties in other countries, is going through a sort of modified "Third Period" development today, for analogous reasons.) The revolution was officially announced to be just around the corner. Roosevelt was a fascist. The A.F. of L. and all of its trade unions were fascist, and the party line was to split the unions to form dual "Red" unions, like the National Miners Union. The socialists were another kind of fascists, called "social-fascists." There was nothing more important than to destroy their organizations, and no united front with them was permissible — except something called "the United Front from Below," which meant that "honest" socialist rank-and-filers were called on to support Communist activities in defiance of their own "social-fascist" leaders. Of all socialists, the left-wing socialists were the worst "social-fascists" of all. Party organizations were oriented toward underground secrecy whether necessary or no, and discipline was conceived in military terms.

The "Third Period" line was still going strong as official policy in 1931 and 1932, when the student movement got started. In 1933 the Communist International was giving signs of softening the line; by 1934 it was clearly on the way out; and in 1935 the decisive flipflop took place when the Franco-Soviet military assistance pact was signed in May. (The French Communist party began voting for war budgets and militarization, and the line spread to other countries immediately.) Later that year, the new Popular Front line was formally inaugurated at the Seventh Congress of the Comintern.

The Popular Front line meant a 180-degree swing in Communist policy from ultra-left to ultra-right. It, like the preceding course, was decisively motivated by Moscow's orientation in foreign policy. Having helped to stymie resistance to Hitler's seizure of power, the Kremlin now took fright at the Nazis' threats of a holy war against Communism. The widest possible military alliance against Germany, in anticipation of World War II, became the crash-program objective, to which all other considerations were subordinated. To push this perspective, the American Communist party, like others, spared no effort to convince Washington and the American power structure that Moscow, together with the Communist parties it kept in tow, was no longer a Red Menace, no longer even interested in revolution. That, in fact, it could be depended on as a respectable defender of the status quo — as long as America participated in a system of "collective security" (world bloc) against the danger from Hitler's Germany that might conceivably serve to "defend the Soviet Union" from attack from that quarter. All pretense at prosecuting a Leninist class-struggle policy was sold out in exchange for wooing the government into a foreign policy satisfactory to Moscow, naturally under anti-Nazi slogans.

Before the Popular Front period was over, nothing was too extreme for the Communist party to use to destroy its image as a Red Menace, including the dissolution of the party itself into a "Communist Political Association." Every bit of radical language in the Communists' program and propaganda was carefully translated into vague liberalese or unceremoniously abandoned or repudiated. The slogan became "Communism is Twentieth Century Americanism," and quotations from Marx and Lenin gave way to passages from Jefferson or Franklin or folksy evocations of Abraham Lincoln. President Roosevelt was transmogrified from a sinister fascist into a People's Hero, and every good Communist became the most fanatical New Dealer within ten miles. Communist front organizations were hastily re-tailored to the new style: for example, the "anti-imperialist" American League Against War and

Fascism became the pro–"collective-security" American League for Peace and Democracy.

Not all of this happened at once. For example, by early 1936 when the Communist party nominated Earl Browder for President, the new line had not yet completely crystallized, but by fall it was clear that the party was advocating a vote for Roosevelt. Since Browder continued formally to run, the Communist press of September–October, 1936 presented one of the weirdest pictures in its checkered history.

While the Communist party was moving all the way right with bewildering speed, the Socialist party, as we have seen, was steadily going left. In 1936, for example, the Socialist party adopted statements against the danger of imperialist war and for a revolutionary transformation of American capitalism which marked an extreme leftward point for the movement, with the approval even of Norman Thomas. (Incidentally, Thomas was no longer a "fascist" or "social-fascist" in Communist treatments. He was now more likely to be denounced as an ultra-left adventuristic Trotskyite.) The YPSL was one of the important ingredients in the leftward pressure within the Socialist party, and pushed for more. Politically speaking, the Socialists and Communists crossed each other, going in opposite directions.

During the first part of the Popular Front period (1935–36), the obsessive concern of the Communist party was for "unity" with the Socialists in any way whatsoever. (This too was an internationalization of the Communist parties' course in Europe, where unity with the mass social-democratic parties could bring the desired respectability.) But by 1937–38 the Communists passed beyond this stage to wooing the real powers of the Establishment, from the Democratic party machines to the National Association of Manufacturers, about whom Browder made unctuous speeches "holding out the hand of friendship" to the "progressive capitalists" who understood the Menace of Hitlerism. Popular Front changed to "Democratic Front" and then to "National Front," as also in Europe where the Italian Communists reached the point of offering common cause with Mussolini's "good" fascists as against the bad Nazi fascists.

This part of the story came to an end with the Hitler-Stalin Pact of 1939, which gave the green light to the Nazis' launching of the Second World War. The nature of the Communists' concern with the menace of Hitlerism was adequately demonstrated when Molotov announced that "fascism is a matter of taste." But this was politically inconceivable to the student movement that was built during the "Third Period" and Popular Front days.

4

We can now return to the year 1931, when the student movement was beginning to stir. This was still in the murky depths of the fantastic "Third Period" line of the communist movement; and naturally the Young Communist League (YCL) was a tiny organization. The YCL's leadership, typified by Gil Green, had been handpicked for woodenheaded docility to the party line, now that every slightly critical element had been driven out as a "Trotskyite" or "Lovestoneite."

This leadership had no interest in orienting toward the organization of students, who were "petty-bourgeois" by definition and unstable intellectuals by occupation (just the kind who had caused so much trouble in the recent factional splits and expulsions). The "Third Period" dogma was that Communists were interested only in "proletarians," although the interest was not reciprocal, and the YCL leaders flatly feared intellectuals, with whom they could not cope in any discussion of their own phantasmagorical politics.

It can be flatly stated that the YCL did not initiate the organization of the National Student League (NSL) and did not want it. Yet it is also true that the NSL was formed by communist students. That these two statements are both true is a testimonial to the misleading simplism of the "conspiracy" theory of radical history.

In New York, where it got started, there were two hostile groups of communist students. The YCL hard-liners, in agreement with their leaders, simply went to school and then hurried away to do their stint for the party or the International Workers Order or one of the other party fronts. The other group, consisting of some YCL'ers and a number of Communist sympathizers and fellow-travelers, held to a "student orientation"; that is, they believed in the possibility and utility of Communist organization of students on campus, in the teeth of the party line.

It was the latter group which initiated the New York Student League (predecessor of the National Student League), while the YCL leadership remained cold to the enterprise but did not prohibit the participation of YCL members in it. It was not until 1933 that the leaders went over wholeheartedly to the "student orientation," in part because of the salient success it had scored in making student Communists through the NSL's activities, and in part because (as we have mentioned) the "Third Period" line was already thawing by this time. By 1934 if not before, there was a complete rapprochement between the strategy and tactics of the YCL factions and the course of the NSL leaders; in fact, in this year the YCL inaugurated a comparable project of its own in the shape of the American Youth Congress.

The only teacher prominent in the organization of the National Student League was a young economics instructor at Columbia named Donald Henderson, who became the NSL's first executive secretary. When the university refused to renew his contract, a student strike on campus made the case a *cause célèbre*. (He later threw himself into work for the Communist-dominated Farm Equipment Workers Union, which absorbed his energies until his death.)

The NSL was one of the most successful of the Communist-led movements of the thirties, and it was also one of the most competently led. Among its top leaders were Joseph Starobin, Joseph Cohen (Joseph Clark), James Wechsler – all of New York – and, from the West Coast, Serril Gerber and Celeste Strack. In general, they were more imaginative and less muscle-bound in style than the cliché-ridden hacks who presided over other Communist party enterprises in the earlier years; in a real sense the NSL pioneered the Popular Front pattern which, after 1935, paid off so well for the communist movement.

One of the first attention-drawing actions of the NSL was its sponsorship of a student delegation to Harlan County, Kentucky, where a desperate miners' strike was taking place, under the aegis of the National Miners Union, against brutal conditions and "legal" terror. The students were turned back from Harlan County by armed intimidation—in a manner somewhat reminiscent of what happened in the sixties to the Freedom Riders in the South. This was not the only attempt by student leaders to link the student movement with the labor movement (as their ideology demanded) but no other case garnered so much notice.

Then in 1932 came the Reed Harris case. Harris, the crusading liberal editor of the Columbia *Spectator*, ran stories exposing the bad conditions in the campus dining hall with regard to the preparation of food and treatment of student waiters. He was clumsily expelled, in the course of a series of events which highlighted the high-handedness and hypocrisy of the Columbia administration. (There have been some parallels since then.) This was the administration of Nicholas Murray Butler—"Nicholas Miraculous Butler," he was called—who was widely thought to have his eyes fixed on tenancy in the White House rather than Morningside Heights. Harris' expulsion precipitated a sort of small-scale free speech movement, with thousands of students coming out in a one-day strike to manifest their indignant protest. The result was mainly a victory; Harris was reinstated, although he had first to make some concessions. The affair was a boost to the NSL, which had organized and led it, and to the student movement in general, particularly in New York City.

The arrival of the Roosevelt administration in 1933 had the effect of heightening political consciousness among the students, as it also did among the general population. A "National Conference of Students in Politics," sponsored by the SLID, took advantage of and reflected this development. The NSL participated in it too, as did the student divisions of the YMCA and YWCA, student Christian associations, and some student service groups. There was a substantial list of eminent professors who allowed their names to be used as sponsors: Charles Beard, Morris R. Cohen, Jerome Davis, John Dewey, and Reinhold Niebuhr. Politicians on the list included Norman Thomas, Philip La Follette, and two senators. It was typical of such gatherings that, although there was a large number of liberals present, it was the Socialists and Communists whose discussions (and disputes) dominated the proceedings, not (in this case) by manipulation but simply because the liberals had nothing distinctive to say. They tended to follow in the wake of the radicals, who set the ideological tone.

5

Perhaps the greatest impetus to the student movement came from the war question.

There is no question but that there has never been a generation of youth more concerned about the danger of war than this one. Their attitude toward this danger was unmistakable: some of the polls and surveys showed a depth of opposition among large masses of youth which was unprecedented. In 1933 a sampling of 920 Columbia students included 31 per cent who considered themselves absolute pacifists—almost one-third; another 52 per cent stated they would bear arms only if the country were invaded; only 8 per cent said they were willing to fight for the United States under any circumstances. A national poll showed 39 per cent who said they would not participate in any war, and another 33 per cent who would do so only if the United States were invaded.

The students obviously did not share the attitude of some of their mentors, like the Fordham dean who denounced student anti-war activity with these words: "They are making fools of themselves. . . . What war are they worrying about anyway?"

The mounting consciousness of the danger of war crystallized politically around the "Oxford Pledge," an English import. In February, 1933 the Oxford Union, following a debate, had passed a resolution which announced that under no circumstances would they "fight for King and country." This was adopted by a vote of 273 to 153; when Randolph Churchill made a motion at the next meeting to expunge this offense to patriotism, the pledge was sustained by an even higher vote, 750 to 175. The sentiment was echoed at other English universities, including Leicester, Manchester, and Cambridge.

In the United States the Oxford Pledge, while retaining the name, was quickly translated into American as a refusal "to support the United States government in any war it may conduct." For the next period the Oxford Pledge was the platform of the student anti-war movement.

It will be noted that the American version does not say quite the same thing as the Oxford version of the Oxford Pledge. The difference was deliberate. It was formulated here by student leaders who, both Socialist and Communist, regarded themselves as Marxists and did not want to make the pledge a statement of absolute pacifism—a viewpoint which was virtually nonexistent among the Communist leaders of the NSL and infrequent in the leadership of the SLID nationally or locally. Hence the American pledge was pointedly *not* worded to read as a refusal "to support any war which the U.S. government might conduct." Instead, it was politically directed against support of the *government* in any war.

In 1934 the two radical student organizations launched what seemed to many at first a rather wild idea, but which turned out to be the most successful single action of the movement: a "Student Strike Against War." The date was set to commemorate the entrance of the United States into the World War, and it took place on April 13, 1934. It was actually only a "demonstration strike," scheduled for one hour, from 11:00 to noon, but it did call on all students to "walk out" of their classrooms. (This was intended literally; students were asked not to cut classes but to go to their scheduled class and leave with as many others as possible.)

At this point the political orbits of the Socialist and Communist students were at perigee. The Communists had already pulled out of the "revolutionary" buffoonery of the "Third Period" but had not yet entered on the complete abandonment of revolutionary tactics which was going to characterize the Popular Front period. On their side, not only the YPSL but even the Socialist party itself had adopted resolutions on the war question which were thoroughly revolutionary-socialist in content and phraseology (in fact, this was one of the main reasons why its "Old Guard" right wing split away). If, as we have said, the Socialists and Communists were crossing each other as they went in opposite political directions, it was during the period from 1934 to the middle of 1935 that they were closest.

There was therefore little difficulty in achieving complete NSL-SLID cooperation in the organization of the first student anti-war strike. To the surprise of its sponsors, it also achieved a considerable measure of success, especially in its public impact. In spite of a barrage of threats and pressure from administrations, about 25,000 students participated in 1934. To be sure, about 15,000 of these were in New York City – and of these, in turn, nearly half were probably accounted for by the three city colleges, City College of New York (CCNY), Brooklyn College, and Hunter. At other campuses the number was not impressive as yet, but the public sat up and took notice. Attempts to intimidate the student strikers at CCNY, Harvard, and Johns Hopkins added to the headlines.

The number of participants took a big jump on April 12 of the following year. The second Student Strike Against War in 1935 – focused, like the first, on the Oxford Pledge – drew about 150,000 students nationally, according to the student organizations. This claim was probably not much exaggerated provided one notes the qualification that not all of these 150,000 actually participated in a "strike," that is, a walk-out from classes. In some places a more usual form of demonstration or meeting was substituted.

The figures were still highest in New York City, with Brooklyn College easily leading again with 6,000; CCNY and Columbia each had 3,500 out. Philadelphia did well, with 3,000 at the University of Pennsylvania and 2,500 at Temple. In the Middle West, the biggest strikes took place at the Universities of Chicago, Minnesota, and Wisconsin. On the West Coast, Berkeley came in, at 4,000, with the second largest demonstration in the country; but even Stanford had 1,500. This time the movement was nationwide: there was some kind of manifestation on over 130 campuses in all regions of the country, including nearly 20 in the South.

This was a great shot in the arm for the student movement, but the fact is that this image of a national mass movement had been projected by the work of comparatively small groups of radical students. To take the example of my own campus, Brooklyn College, which had seen the largest strike in the country for both years: there were probably about thirty active members each in both the SLID and NSL chapters, give or take another dozen. If about 95 per cent of the student body came out on the strike, in the face of administration threats of disciplinary action and the violent opposition of the student newspaper, this was an index not to the size of the *direct* organizational influence of either group but rather to the climate of social and political opinion among the students generally. I doubt whether there was at any time during this period a number of student-movement activists greater than there are today (1965), though there are two important qualifications to be added: the total student population in the universities and colleges was much smaller then and the student leaderships insisted on more compact and efficient organization than is common today. The main difference was in the times.

6

The years 1934–35 were not only those in which the Communists and Socialists came closest together politically, but also those in which the Communists, having abandoned the doctrine that Socialists were "social-fascists," started going all-out for "unity" with those whom it had so recently stigmatized. On the student field, the NSL started proposing unity with the SLID in 1934. With cooperation in two student strikes behind them, and increasing cooperation in other projects, the SLID began to look favorably upon the proposal. By 1935, as their own line toward "unity" blossomed internationally, the Communists seemed ready to make almost any concession to get agreement. Within the SLID, the left-wing YPSL also was favorable to merger, feeling that in a united student movement their own politics would have a larger field to operate in. Another source of pressure toward merger was the growth of the NSL, which threatened to overshadow the SLID.

In June the national executive committee of the SLID voted for fusion, and the unity convention was held during Christmas week in Columbus, Ohio. The new organization formed there was called the American Student Union.

There was a considerable bloc of previously unaffiliated liberals at this convention, but, as before, they played no independent role. The agreements, disputes, and discussions emanated from the Socialist and Communist blocs. By this time, not only the Franco-Soviet Pact but also the speeches and documents of the Seventh Congress of the Comintern had begun to make clear the direction of the Popular Front policy. The entire international Communist movement, including the American party with its usual automatism, had already by this time abandoned its anti-war policy and, in all countries earmarked for the anti-German alliance, was headed in the direction of classic jingoism. Soon there were going to be no more shrill "patriots" than the Communists.

The NSL line had not yet been overtly affected. Even though, outside the student field, the Young Communist League had dutifully made clear that the Oxford Pledge was now obsolete, the leaders of the NSL formally stated that the Oxford Pledge would be maintained, in answer to a challenge from the Socialists. In fact the process of coordinating the student movement with the new Communist pro-war line was going to take two years, up to the Vassar convention of the ASU at Christmastime 1937, whereas elsewhere Communist-dominated organizations were able to carry out the flipflop in weeks or months. The difference was due entirely to the bitter fight made against this turn by the Yipsel forces in the SLID.

At the fusion convention, therefore, all was not sweetness and light, as might have been the case if the merger had taken place a few months earlier. One sticky question was the attitude of the ASU toward the Russian regime. In a compromise, a resolution referred to the Soviet Union only as an example of a "non-imperialist" nation whose "peace policy" deserved support—a formulation which was then satisfactory to the left-wing Socialists too. Another problem, the relationship of the ASU to the Communist front organization which then still called itself the American League Against War and Fascism, was settled by an agreement not to affiliate with any such body except by a three-quarters vote of the national committee.

The main dispute took place over the question of war policy. In line with the preconvention pledge of the NSL leadership, the Oxford Pledge was re-endorsed, by a vote of 244–49 (the 49 were liberals who agreed with the *new* Communist line of "collective security" and had no reason to weasel over it). But when the Socialist bloc introduced a resolution which included the idea that the Oxford Pledge would still be applicable even if the United States were aligned with Russia in the war-for-democracy toward which the Communists now looked, this was defeated 155–193 by the combined votes of the Communists and pro–collective-security liberals against the Socialist left wing. But this was still only a negative action, as compared with the later complete endorsement of American foreign policy when the ASU came under unchallenged Communist domination.

The leadership of the new organization was divided according to preconvention agreement. Three "LID types" became national officers: Lash as executive secretary, George Edwards as national chairman, and Molly Yard as treasurer. NSL'ers took the posts of high school chairman, field secretary, and editor of the magazine (*Student Advocate*). The national committee was divided into three blocs, with an equal number named by the SLID and NSL, leaving a number of seats for "unaffiliated liberals." There was only one hitch in these proceedings: the morning of the vote, the YCL faction decided that they would not accept one name on the SLID list—mine—in spite of the previous agreement that each of the merging organizations would name its own people to the national committee. The infuriated SLID'ers informed them that this would explode the agreement, and the YCL finally backed down, muttering darkly about the "disruptive" role I had played by presenting the Socialist anti-war resolution on the Oxford Pledge.

7

The typical issues on which the student movement fought and around which it organized were mainly the following six, given roughly in order of importance:

(1) Anti-war activity and opposition to compulsory ROTC.

(2) Violations of academic freedom and student rights on campus.

(3) Issues involving economic aid to students (tuition fees, free textbooks, etc.).

(4) Reform of college administrations, particularly changes in the boards of trustees who ruled the campuses.

(5) Aid to the labor movement.

(6) Anti-fascist activity—which could be concretized only now and then, as when a delegation of Italian Fascist student leaders were welcomed at CCNY by the administration in one way and by the student body in another.

There were, of course, the usual cries of alarm from all quarters as the student movement grew and impressed the public mind with the fact that something was happening in the colleges. The pulp writer H. Bedford-Jones—emulating Calvin Coolidge's 1921 article, "Are the Reds Stalking Our College Women?"—published an article in *Liberty* under the pen name of J. G. Shaw, asking "Will the Communists Get Our Girls in College?", purporting to explain the terrible dangers to which his daughter had been subjected by sinister Red conspirators. The following week the *New Masses* headlined a reply, "My Father Is a Liar!", by Nancy Bedford-Jones, the daughter, who shortly thereafter atoned for her sins by marrying Lash.

A recurrent image of the student movement of the thirties as "ideological" rather than "activist" needs qualification. It certainly was "ideological," being under the thorough leadership of Communists and Socialists, but it was also at least as "activist" as campus radicals today; the difference was that it did not counterpose one to the other. Probably all wings would have agreed on the following statement from the SLID's *Blueprints for Action—A Handbook for Student Revolutionists*: "The radical movement has too many sideline commentators; the great need is for participants. Besides, action is one of the best ways of getting clarification."

But the second period of the student movement was now beginning, in which the highly ideological leadership of the Communist students made a turn toward "de-ideologizing" and depoliticalizing the movement in line with their new orientation. The "non-ideological" mask that was to be adopted was incompatible even with ideology in a liberal form. What was beginning was the cant of speaking in the name of "The Students," whose aspirations and most secret thoughts always somehow coincided with the latest pronouncements of the YCL. Already before the ASU merger convention, the *NSL Organizer* (organizational bulletin) for December, 1935 had inveighed against the belief that the new student organization would be "radical": "For what purpose is the Union formed? We say, simply, to protect our welfare, to advance our interests, to give us strength. Then why do some NSL'ers still view the Union in terms of the 'radical,' 'liberal,' 'liberal-radical' etc. students in their particular schools? Is it not because these NSL'ers see the Union primarily in terms of vague 'social problems,' political discussions, etc., and not in terms of student problems, campus issues."[3] This dichotomy between "social problems" and "student problems, campus issues" was a fraudulent one, for the approach of the NSL – as of the SLID – had been to direct activity and education to bridging the gap between the two, showing the connection between campus issues and broader social problems, and the relevance of society-wide radical solutions to student life. What the NSL-YCL line was now demanding was the dropping of an overtly radical approach to *both* social problems and campus issues, in the interest of maximum unity of all men of good will for an anti-German alliance.

This was acted out most obviously in the student anti-war actions of 1936 and 1937. There were two influences at work now, only one of which was the new Communist line against militancy. The other was that many of the campus administrations sharply changed their tone. Instead of denouncing the strike and threatening draconic punishment, they rolled with the punch and tried to clinch. They offered auditorium facilities, called off classes for the hour, and proposed to make it all official: only, of course, "why should it be called a strike, since you aren't really striking against us, are you?" And "anti-war" is *so* negative: why not "for peace?" Increasingly, "Peace Assemblies" replaced the anti-war strikes, and, swathed in respectability, the students listened to peaceful rhetoric in the same pews where they were accustomed to hearing commencement addresses.

The Communists eagerly accepted every such offer by administrations, and the statistics of participants rose mightily, as whole campuses went through the mo-

[3] *NSL Organizer*, December, 1935.

tions of a "Peace Assembly." There were strikes of the 1934–35 variety, and evocations of the Oxford Pledge, mainly in those places where the left-wing Socialists dominated the ASU chapter. Liberal students in the ASU followed in the wake of the Communist line, which suited them to a T; in fact, they could feel, with justice, that it was the Communist line which had come over to them, not the other way around. By 1937 the guts had been taken out of what had once been the Student Strike Against War.

At the Christmas 1936 convention of the ASU, the time was not yet propitious to unload the Oxford Pledge formally, as was shown by the fact that a YPSL-sponsored resolution attacking the collective-security (pro-war) line lost by only thirty-seven votes. What did happen, however, was that the two "LID types" who had become ASU national officers, Lash and Yard, went over to the Popular Front and collective-security line and became staunch fellow-travelers of the Communist bloc. At a Socialist caucus meeting during the convention itself, a furious denunciation of these two was the main feature, and in effect the national staff of the ASU became monolithic.

During 1937 pro-war feeling in the country grew apace. The New Deal moved more openly toward interventionism, as Roosevelt came out in October with his "Quarantine the Aggressor" speech. The Socialist anti-war minority in the ASU had a harder row to hoe. By the end of 1937 the Communists, in bloc with Lash, were in position to dump the last vestiges of the student movement's militant politics and anti-war activity. At the convention, a well-organized Socialist bloc of delegates carried on a last-ditch fight to save the Oxford

Pledge, but lost, 282–108. By the 1938 convention, with the Socialist left wing out, the complete Popular-Frontization of the organization bore fruit: the Roosevelt administration finally gave its official blessing to the ASU, in a letter of greetings to the convention from the President; the convention also got messages from the mayor of New York and its Board of Higher Education, from the president of CCNY, from the women's director of the Democratic National Committee, and other notables. The student movement was now completely respectable, completely pro-administration, and completely emasculated.

The new atmosphere that enveloped the ASU can be gathered, in part, from the following comment by a friend of the movement, Bruce Bliven, writing in the *New Republic* for January 11, 1939 on the convention that had just taken place:

> Their enthusiasm reached its peak at the Jamboree in the huge jai-alai auditorium of the Hippodrome (seating capacity 4500) which was filled to its loftiest tier. There were a quintet of white-flanneled cheer leaders, a swing band, and shaggers doing the Campus Stomp ("everybody's doing it, ASU'ing it") – confetti. There were ASU feathers and buttons, a brief musical comedy by the Mob Theatre and pretty ushers in academic caps and gowns. All the trappings of a big-game rally were present and the difference was that they were cheering, not the Crimson to beat the Blue, but Democracy to beat Reaction. To me, it bordered just alongside the phoney.[4]

It *was* phoney, of course, whatever one might think of football-rally exercises. This was making like Joe College according to the detailed instructions of the *YCL Organizer* on "How to Be American."

[4] Bruce Bliven, *New Republic*, January 11, 1939.

Later on in 1939 there was a second excellent example of what had happened. This one is directly from the *Young Communist League Bulletin* at the University of Wisconsin: "Some people have the idea that a YCL'er is politically minded, that nothing outside of politics means anything. Gosh, no. They have a few simple problems. There is the problem of getting good men on the baseball team this spring, of opposition from other pingpong teams, of dating girls, etc. We go to shows, parties, dances, and all that. In short, the YCL and its members are no different from other people except that we believe in dialectical materialism as the solution to all problems."[5]

This is what the student movement had become. The last chapter was written after September, 1939. After four years of eviscerating the student anti-war movement for the sake of the grand alliance against Nazism, the Second World War was inaugurated with the Hitler-Stalin Pact. The Communist leaders of the ASU ground all gears into reverse, and some of the passengers got shaken out, particularly Lash, who really believed what he had been saying about collective security. At the Christmas 1939 convention, the rug was pulled from under the "innocents." The Communists held it in iron control, rolling up huge majorities even on procedural questions whenever necessary. A motion condemning the Soviet attack on Finland was defeated 322–49. It was announced that the war was "imperialist," and ASU propaganda echoed the slogan that "The Yanks Are Not Coming." A motion for a national membership referen-

[5] *Young Communist League Bulletin*, University of Wisconsin, 1939.

dum on this line was overwhelmingly turned down. Lash was replaced in the executive secretary's office by the YCL apparatus-man, Bert Witt. At the 1940 convention there was no opposition at all—also no cheerleaders, confetti, or shaggers; the major speakers were all Communists or fellow-travelers. But by this time it scarcely mattered, for the ASU was a shell. When the line changed again, after the German attack on Russia, and the Communists became shrill patriots again, it was too late to save the student movement even in its Popular Front form. The student movement was dead.

8

This is not the place to attempt a full assessment of the impact of the student movement of the thirties, but a word must be said about one type of assessment that has been published. This latter is based on the fact, which I have stressed in connection with the anti-war strike, that there was always a great disparity between the number who actually joined any of the radical student organizations and the larger number who could be moved into action by this small vanguard. Two writers on the subject have operated with the statistics in a manner which is a model of how not to understand social movements.

One is Robert W. Iversen who, in his *The Communists and the Schools*, makes a characteristic remark. When the alumni of CCNY were disturbed by the college's "red" reputation—"The Alumni Association reassured them in 1936 that only 1 per cent of the students belonged to radical organizations. But unfortunately, the 99 per cent possessed few of the gifts for publicity that seemed the peculiar talent of the dedicated few."[6]

This reduction of the radical students' appeal to a "peculiar talent" for clever publicity makes a mystery where there was none. It would be hard to explain how assiduous reading of Marx and Lenin gave rise to this gift. But the radical students at CCNY needed no Madison Avenue gifts when they had a college president like Frederick B. Robinson, a president who could personally make an umbrella-swinging physical attack on a student protest meeting (1933); who first insisted on subjecting the student body to a college reception for an official delegation of Italian Fascist students, and then reacted to the hissing of his guests with an uncontrolled outburst of "Guttersnipes!" (1934). These were only two of his more dramatic exploits, guaranteed equally to make headlines and to convince unaligned students that they had to take a stand. (CCNY blossomed with lapel buttons reading "I Am a Guttersnipe.")

Even without such cooperation by administrations gifted with a peculiar talent for alienating their students—especially under the pressure of conservative forces off-campus—Iversen's dichotomy between the "1 per cent" and the "99 per cent" is a basic misunderstanding of the relationship of forces. Around the 1 per cent who actually joined a radical student group were concentric rings of influence, embracing different portions of the student body as different forms of commitment were demanded. For every one who joined there were perhaps two who agreed in the main with what the

[6] Robert W. Iversen, *The Communists and the Schools* (New York: Harcourt, Brace and World, Inc., 1959).

student movement was trying to do, but who did not join, either for lack of time to devote to such activity or for other reasons which did them less credit. There was another circle of students who were ready to support most of the campaigns or actions which the student organizations might launch on a given issue, such as defense of students victimized by the administration. It was probably most inclusive during the annual anti-war actions, whether in the form of the anti-war strike or the "peace assembly."

Even outside the widest of these concentric circles, if we consider the students who never participated in any dissenting form of activity at all, it would be an error to suppose that all of them were hostile to the student movement and needed only adequate talents for publicity to make this hostility felt. The general social disillusionment with the status quo, with "The System," conditioned many of them, if only because it put them on the defensive before the self-confident radicals. It deprived them of that capacity to feel that "all radicals must be kooks," which is characteristic of a social system sure of itself.

The picture, then, is far more complex than a "1 per cent" versus a "99 per cent," and it was through this complexity that the organized student movement made itself felt as a relatively small vanguard which, from time to time, could put much larger masses into motion.

Iversen's handling of statistics reflects a profound ignorance of what was going on at the time. Thus he writes:

> In 1941, a careful attempt was made to assess the extent of communism among the students of Brooklyn College and City College during the previous five years. The most re-

liable index was found to be the Communist vote in student elections. Thus, at the peak of Communist power in 1938, 1,002 votes were cast in a Brooklyn College straw ballet. Of this number, 280 were cast for the Communist candidate. Several things may be concluded from this: first, since the total college enrollment was over 10,000, the political indifference of the vast majority of students was virtually monumental, with the Communists comprising less than 3 per cent of the total student body. The figures do show, however, that about one-third of the students who were politically conscious enough to vote at all voted Communist.[7]

What is left entirely out of the picture is the fact that in 1938, after some years of intensive Communist propaganda identifying the Popular Front line with euphoric enthusiasm for the New Deal, and particularly in 1938 when Roosevelt was obviously steering an interventionist course, there were far more Communist sympathizers and fellow-travelers who voted for the New Deal candidates than there were Communist party members who registered their vote for the ceremonial candidates put up by the party. It would be impossible to pick a year which would be worse than 1938 for determining pro-Communist sympathies on the basis of casting a ballot for the party's candidates.

Iversen's passage continues as follows, with a second case: "At City College, the situation was somewhat different. In a straw vote held during the presidential campaign of 1940, there were only 126 Communist votes out of a total of 2,656. The enrollment at City was about 6,000. City College thus reveals. . . ."[8] But it does not matter what Iversen thinks it reveals, since he seems to be unconcerned about, and does not mention, the fact that this straw poll took place after one year of the Nazi-

[7] *Ibid.* [8] *Ibid.*

Soviet pact. The Communist power was now an ally of Hitler – especially in the eyes of a City College student body with a very high proportion of Jewish students. By this time the Communist party itself was staggering, and especially its sympathizers were falling away in droves. The marked difference between Brooklyn College in 1938 and City College in 1940 depends on the background politics, not on the place.

However, Iversen's subject, the influence of Communists in the colleges, is only a part of the larger problem of the relation of the student movement to the campus. A similar approach is taken, in a more impressionistic fashion, by Murray Kempton in a book about the thirties, *Part of Our Time*, which makes some remarks about the student movement in its last chapter.

Kempton recalls that in *Harper's* of August, 1931, just before the student movement blossomed before the public, Harold J. Laski had published an article whose title asked: "Why Don't Your Young People Care?" The question, asserts Kempton, "was not materially less valid" at the fever pitch of the student movement in 1937 than it had been in 1931, and he cites statistics to indicate this:

> At the height of its uproar, the ASU had only twelve thousand members and claimed another eight thousand who hadn't paid their dues but were otherwise totally committed. The Young Communist League had fewer than five thousand student members at any one time. As the thirties wore on, the Young People's Socialist League, the heroic and historic Yipsels, fell below one thousand members[9] and the Young Trotskyites below five hundred.

[9] But this was true only after the split in the socialist movement which took place toward the end of 1937. For 1935–37, which is the "fever-pitch" Kempton is presumably considering, the YPSL probably had a couple of thousand members or more.

Yet the few persons in those last three organizations made most of the history of student rebellion in the thirties. In 1937, as an instance, young Communists, young Socialists, and one young Trotskyite constituted eighteen of the thirty members of the National Executive Committee of the American Student Union; and all its national officers were either Socialists or Communists. There were close to four million high school and college students in the United States in 1937; the myth of their radical impulse was created, at the very most, by fifteen thousand persons. It has been said that these fifteen thousand set the tone for the American campus in the thirties, in which case they did it by default. A tone set by three-tenths of one per cent of a community can hardly, after all, be described as a tone.[10]

The problem of how a "tone" is set by the relationship between a small minority of activists and a larger mass of sympathetic or impressionable students is, as I have already discussed, more complex than such statistics can express. However, Kempton's tendentiousness is manifested by his use of the figure "four million high school and college students." No one has ever claimed that the student movement set the tone in the high schools; it was remarkable enough that fairly active movements of high school students *were* built during the thirties, at least in New York and Chicago. It is a question, therefore, of about a million and a quarter college students; and even here we must remember that most institutions of higher education, especially the small freshwater colleges, denominational schools, and vocational-technical institutions in nonurban areas, remained little affected by the swirl of events—any events. Nor need it be claimed that the student movement set the tone at, say, Harvard if the totality of university life is thereby meant.

[10] Murray Kempton, *Part of Our Time* (New York: Simon and Schuster, Inc., 1955).

In fact, the same point could quite legitimately be made even about what was probably the most highly politicalized college in the country, Brooklyn College, during the time I was chairman of its SLID chapter as well as in the subsequent years. The large majority of students devoted themselves to studying and getting their sheepskins and pursuing their personal lives just as if there were no student movement, but even while doing so they could not help absorbing the climate of ideas which pervaded the *political* life of the campus as a part of the larger society. Now, the tone which was set by the small vanguard of student activists was precisely this *political* tone, through all of the concentric circles which I have described.

Here is a final example, from Kempton, of how easy it is to get three mistakes into three sentences: "What history there is asserts that in 1937 half a million American college students took an oath never to support this government in any war. The Selective Service Act came three and one-half years later; fewer than one hundred men refused to register under it as a matter of principle. By 1943, just 1,400 young men of all sorts had gone to prison for ideological or ethical defiance of the draft law. And half of those were Jehovah's Witnesses. . . .[11]

In the first place, the Oxford Pledge was not an oath to become a conscientious objector, as I have explained. With few exceptions, the Socialists and Communists who led the student movement were vigorously and articulately opposed to conscientious objection as a policy (the *right* to conscientious objection is another matter), and did not advocate that revolutionary students go to jail rather than accept the draft. Second, it is not true,

[11] *Ibid.*

nor was it claimed, that "half a million American college students" took the Oxford Pledge in 1937. That figure is for total participants in the various "peace assemblies" or other anti-war demonstrations that took place in 1937. And, as has been related, by this time the Oxford Pledge had been dumped in practice by the ASU leadership and most chapters, preparatory to being officially dumped at the Christmas convention. This already suggests the third and most important error. Kempton writes as if the student movement rejected the coming war until it came, and then the movement collapsed. Like Iversen, he ignores the fact that the student movement had been turned into a political instrument for preparing youth to *accept* the war as a crusade against fascism, years before the test came.

The student movement was one of the first casualties of the Second World War, but its impact was not ended. For the next couple of decades at least, wherever anything was stirring in the labor movement or in liberal campaigns, wherever there was action for progressive causes or voices were raised in dissent from the Establishment, there one was sure to find alumni of this student movement, who had gotten their political education and organizational training and experience in the American Student Union or the Student League for Industrial Democracy or the National Student League. The history we have sketched is that of one of the most important educational institutions of twentieth-century America.

BURTON K. WHEELER

My Years with Roosevelt

Introduction by Sheldon Plager

Burton Kendall Wheeler, sometime Democrat, was born in Hudson, Massachusetts, February 27, 1882. He grew up there, and then, in keeping with the admonitions of the times, went west. He went first to Michigan where he did his law work at the University of Michigan, graduating in 1905. He continued west to Silver Bow County, Montana, and after an interim period of some traveling, he eventually settled in the town of Butte and began the practice of law.

In 1910 Burton Wheeler was elected to the state house of representatives. He became United States District Attorney for Montana in 1913, serving until 1918. His years as district attorney were marked by general public agitation. This was the time of the I.W.W., the labor strikes, and the pacifist demonstrations. Senator Wheeler, attorney Wheeler at that time, declined in several cases to take action against these alleged "rabble-rousers"; and indeed he suggested at one

Sheldon Plager is a professor in the College of Law, University of Illinois.

point that the mine owners themselves were provoking the strikes to drive up the price of copper. All of this earned him the reputation in Montana, in some circles at least, of a dangerous radical.

In 1920 Mr. Wheeler ran for governor on a nonpartisan league ticket. The ticket included a Negro and a Blackfoot Indian. It was a Republican year. Two years later, in 1922, he became the Democratic nominee for United States senator and was elected, despite the opposition charges that he wanted to introduce free love into Montana. Perhaps the climate had something to do with the fact that nobody really believed it.

After two years in the Senate, Senator Wheeler left the Democrats and became the unsuccessful candidate for Vice-President and running mate of Robert La Follette on the Progressive ticket.

In 1928, Senator Wheeler, back with the Democrats, was re-elected to the Senate for a second term, and became a strong supporter of Franklin Delano Roosevelt. He toured the West on F.D.R.'s behalf in 1932 and was instrumental in promoting F.D.R.'s candidacy. This, however, did not keep Senator Wheeler from exercising his right of dissent. He publicly opposed the President over the creation of the NRA. He was an early and vigorous critic of the court-packing plan, and finally with the coming of World War II, he fought the President on the repeal of the Arms Embargo and opposed U.S. efforts to rearm the Allies.

Senator Wheeler served continually in the United States Senate from 1928 to 1947. After an unsuccessful race for renomination in 1946, he retired from the Senate and for the last twenty years has practiced law in Washington, D.C., with his son Edward.

MY LONG AND BUMPY POLITICAL RELATIONSHIP with Franklin D. Roosevelt began in the Hotel Commodore in New York City in April, 1930. I was one of the main speakers at the Democratic party's Jefferson Day dinner. I had been reluctant to accept the invitation because the dinner was under the auspices of Tammany Hall, which I disliked, but Senator Robert F. Wagner of New York and Jouett Shouse, executive chairman of the Democratic National Committee, talked me into accepting.

Wagner warned me that long-winded speeches were not appreciated by the bibulous diners. When I saw the bottles on the massed tables and the rapidly liquefying politicians crowded into the ballroom, I was glad I had planned to speak for only fifteen minutes. Also I took the precaution of issuing a press release before the dinner began. I had a serious message – I was coming out for Roosevelt for President. Our speeches were to be carried over the NBC Blue Network, and I did not want my message lost in the 100-proof din enveloping the ballroom. Having been tipped off that I would toss his hat into the ring, Roosevelt tactfully left the hall before I spoke.

Political historians have since recorded that I was the first nationally known Democrat to publicly back Roosevelt for the 1932 nomination. The *New York Times* reported the next day that I had "launched a boom for the governor." I was for Roosevelt because I felt he could be elected President; also I wanted to head off another race by Al Smith. I was an admirer of Al and felt he had made a great governor of New York. In 1928 I had been anxious to see him elected – and, for a while, I thought he could be.

Roosevelt, playing the game cautiously in 1930, did not thank me for my early endorsement for President until June. Then, he wrote: "I was made very happy by your reference to me at the Democratic club dinner, for the very good reason that I have always thought of you as one of the real leaders of progressive thought and action in this country. Therefore, to be considered as a real progressive by you means something to me."

My first rift with the new President was over the question of silver. I had advocated the coinage of silver during Hoover's administration and continued to do so in Roosevelt's. I had come within one vote of passing it through the Senate. Vice-President Garner reportedly warned FDR that unless he acted in some way on the money issue, my 16-1 proposal would pass the next test. The President called in Senators Jimmy Byrnes, Key Pittman, and a number of others to discuss possible legislation of money. I was conspicuously not invited. I had led the fight for reform.

While the White House conference was in progress, I was standing in the Mayflower Hotel lobby. A friend asked me if I would like to meet Father Coughlin and we went upstairs. The Reverend Charles Edward Coughlin, the famous "radio priest" who was then at the height of his popularity, was pacing up and down his room. As he walked, he told me about the money conference. I asked him if the group planned to include the remonetization of silver in the proposed legislation and he said "no." I told the priest that unless the administration did something about the remonetization of silver I would offer my amendment to any bill that came up, and I was quite critical of Roosevelt.

The next morning Frank Walker, then assistant Democratic chairman and an old Montana friend, telephoned me and said he understood I was on the warpath. I acknowledged that I was. "You can't break with the President," he said. "Oh, yes, I can," I replied. Walker said the President wanted to see me on the silver question. I told him I would not see the President. A little later, Marvin H. McIntyre, Roosevelt's appointments secretary, telephoned me and persuaded me to go to the White House.

FDR's ability to seduce a caller with his special blend of charm and blarney was formidable. Once, at a time when William Randolph Hearst was editorially blasting Roosevelt, I was visiting him in California. I urged him to have a talk with the President. Hearst admitted frankly that he was "afraid to"—because he might be taken in.

When I walked into the Oval Room of the White House, FDR greeted me with a wave of his hand and an airy: "Hello, Burt, I want to talk to you about silver." "Mr. President," I said, "I don't deserve this kind of treatment from you, and I'm not going to take it. You called in all these people, none of whom was sincerely interested in the fight I am making to remonetize silver." "Burt," he replied smoothly, "Bryan killed the remonetization of silver in 1896." "Mr. President," I responded, "if this situation keeps up, it is going to take a lot worse remedies to solve our monetary problem than remonetization of silver."

Though FDR never remonetized silver, he did inflate our currency by cutting the gold content of the dollar, and started a program of buying silver above the market price. That helped the mining campanies. The silver purchase program was all the mining companies were interested in.

Starting my third six-year term in the Senate in January, 1935, I became chairman of the Interstate Commerce Committee. The National Power Policy Committee reported that thirteen holding company groups controlled three-quarters of the privately owned electric utility industry and that the three largest – Electric Bond and Share, United Corporation, and Insull – controlled some 40 per cent themselves. I had gotten up a bill to regulate the holding companies but a day before I planned to introduce it the President called a conference to discuss a promise in his state-of-the-union message to abolish their evils. Present with me were the late Sam Rayburn, then chairman of the House Interstate Commerce Committee, Senators Norris and Borah, and several others including Tommy the Cork.[1]

FDR announced at the meeting that Rayburn would introduce the bill. I felt he did not want me to handle any part of it. I said, "Well, I've got a bill I'm going to introduce." As soon as I got back to my office, Corcoran and Ben Cohen, the White House bill drafting specialist, arrived. They urged me to introduce the administration bill instead of my own. They said I would not have to do anything until after the bill passed the House. I agreed to go along; their bill was more carefully drafted than mine. But over in the House, Rayburn could not seem to get started. I felt that Sam himself was a little tepid about the so-called "death sentence."

The White House then appealed to me to get the bill moving on the Senate side. So I scheduled hearings. I was promptly visited by a utility lobbyist who said: "These utility people feel you're putting a gun at their heads and they're going to destroy anybody that gets in their way." "Did they tell you to give me that message?"

[1] Thomas Corcoran, a close friend and adviser to Franklin Delano Roosevelt.

I asked. "Not exactly," he replied. I asked him to take a message to them. "You tell them," I said, "that a lot of experts have tried to destroy me and haven't been able to get away with it. If these people know any new ways, I hope they'll bring them on – I'd like to see what they are."

A few days later, I was visited by two of their lobbyists. They asked me what I was going to do about the "death sentence." I said I was going to keep it if I could. They wanted to know how much time the utilities would have to present their case. I said I would give them one week and the government one week. "Oh, we've got to have 30 or 40 days," they said. "Well," I said, "if your lawyers can't tell what's wrong with a bill in a week's time, it's just too bad."

I got the bill approved by my committee without much trouble and it reached the Senate floor late in May. One night early in June I was attending a big party given by Joe Kennedy at his Potomac, Maryland, mansion. Quite a few senators were there. About midnight, Jimmy Byrnes pulled me aside. "Burt, you're putting the President on the spot with that so-called 'death sentence,'" he said. I said, "This is the President's bill." "Well, I've talked with the President and had him talked out of it but he said he was standing behind Burt Wheeler," Byrnes replied. "He isn't standing behind me," I said. "I'm standing behind him."

I telephoned the President and said I wanted to see him, and repeated Byrnes's remarks. "Jimmy didn't have any right to say that," he told me. "Well, Mr. President," I said, "don't give the impression you're willing to change, because this is your bill." He said he didn't want to change it.

Senator John H. Bankhead echoed Byrnes's line to me, and so did a few other Southerners. I went back to the White House. FDR was sitting in bed, propped up by pillows, his cigarette and holder jutting up out of his mouth and cigarette ashes dropping on the bedspread. I started right off saying I would change the bill any way he wanted it changed, but that I was tired of being buttonholed by senators. He turned on the charm and reassured me that he was standing pat. I suggested that he make a public statement to clear the air. He didn't want to do that, but he called for a pencil and paper and scrawled a short statement. "You can show this to the boys," he said, giving the sheet of paper to me. He did not intend for me to make it public – I suspected he was being very careful in what he was saying to the utility people privately.

As the debate in the Senate got hot, Senator William H. Dieterich of Illinois rose and insisted that Roosevelt was willing to amend the bill by striking out the "death sentence" provision in Section 11. This is what I had been waiting for. I drew the President's note from my pocket, where I had been keeping it handy, and read it to the Senate.

"*Dear Burt*," it ran, "*to verify my talk with you this morning, I am very clear in my own mind that while clarifying or minor amendments to Sec. 11 cannot be objected to, nevertheless any amendment which goes to the heart of major objectives of Sec. 11 would strike at the heart of the bill itself and is wholly contrary to the recommendations of myself. Sincerely, Franklin D. Roosevelt.*"

That knocked the wind out of the opposition. Section 11 was retained by the hairline margin of 45–44 and the bill itself then easily passed the Senate 56–32. The President telephoned me from Hyde Park to congratulate me, sounding happy about the way the bill had been handled.

On the House side, meanwhile, the Commerce Committee struck out the mandatory death sentence, giving the SEC discretionary power to order dissolution instead. When the two versions of the bill went into a Senate-House conference for the showdown, a deadlock resulted. After a week of stalemate, the President called me and told me I would have to take the bill back to the Senate for another vote. I suggested that he let the bill die in conference and take the case against the utilities to the people. He said he did not want to do that—he wanted something to come out of conference. I told him I would not take the bill back to the Senate. I pointed out that I had gotten the death sentence provision through with a margin of a single vote and that now the opposition could use the conference deadlock to pick up votes and kill the death sentence outright. "What should I do?" he asked. I advised him to call in some of the House leaders who professed to be such great friends of his and tell them to go along with me. I also suggested that he write a letter to Rayburn telling him flatly that he wanted the Senate version passed. Roosevelt asked me to compose such a letter. Barkley and I went back to my office. We drafted the note and the President signed it and had it delivered to Rayburn. The bill was passed in the House.

While I had earlier disagreed with FDR on his veto of the soldiers' bonus, on the silver question, and on the NRA, my first real break with him began on February 5, 1937. In New York, on a mission for the Interstate Commerce Committee, I read in a newspaper that FDR had dropped a political bombshell in Washington. He was asking Congress for a revolutionary and sweeping "reorganization of the judiciary," under which he could then name six new justices.

In May, Corcoran came to me and urged me to introduce a bill which would add three members to the Supreme Court. I asked Tom, who was one of FDR's closest advisers, if he wanted to defeat the President in the 1936 election. I recalled to him that when I ran for Vice-President on Bob La Follette's independent Progressive ticket in 1924 our platform had proposed a limitation on the high bench. It had been used devastatingly against us from one end of the country to the other.

A few days later I got a telephone call from Charley Michelson, publicity director of the Democratic National Committee and an old friend. I stalled off an appointment with him while I worked over a statement on the bill for the press. I released the statement and then had Michelson come to my office. He said the President wanted me to have dinner with him at the White House. "Charley," I said, "I've just given out a statement opposing the packing of the Court. He should save the plate for some of those weak-kneed boys and go after them because he can't do anything with me." I heard no more about dinner at the White House.

Once my statement was in the press, however, Corcoran asked me to lunch. Tommy opened the conversation by saying the President wanted to see me to give me some background on the Court issue. "He doesn't care about those Tories being against it," he explained, "but he doesn't want you to be against it."

Corcoran then made it plain that if I went along with

the Court plan I could sit in on the naming of some of the new justices. "If you don't go along," Corcoran continued, "he'll make a deal with Tammany and the Southerners and he'll put their people on the Court."

I replied that Corcoran was probably right about that but I wasn't going along. When Corcoran angrily warned me that the bill would pass, I pounded the table and replied just as angrily, "Well, Tommy, he *isn't* going to get it! How do you like that!"

A small group of Democrats met at Tydings' house. "Burt, we can't lick it but we'll fight it," Byrd remarked. "Harry, why are you against it?" I asked him. "Because it's wrong in principle," he said. "Well," I replied, "most of the members of the Senate are lawyers. Deep down, they agree with you and me, but they're like a lot of mercenaries. They want patronage. A small army that believes in principle can lick a bunch of mercenaries, and we'll lick them!" Byrd said he was glad I felt that way.

After that a group of Democrats and Republicans met. They selected me as leader of the opposition. We set up a steering committee of eighteen members. Each member was assigned to keep after certain senators who were uncommitted. Assignments were made on the basis of each man's personal acquaintance with those senators. Our steering committee met secretly every day in a Capitol hideaway to alter strategy in the light of shifting events. Our intelligence network was unexpectedly reinforced by reports from inside the administration forces. Leslie Biffle, an officer of the Senate who was ostensibly working for the other side informed me nightly by telephone who was weak on their side and who seemed to be weakening on our side.

One of my problems was trying to keep some corporation lawyers from making statements that would play into Roosevelt's hands. When the fight was just getting underway, I was invited to New York to meet with the president of the New York Bar Association. When I arrived at his office, I found lawyers from eight or ten of the top New York law firms there, including John W. Davis, the 1924 Democratic presidential nominee. They asked me what they could do to help defeat the Court-packing bill.

"Do you really want to help?" I asked. They assured me they would do whatever they could. "Have you any influence with any farm organizations?" I asked. They didn't think so. "Have you any influence with any labor organizations?" "Definitely not." "Have you any influence with church organizations?" "Perhaps some." "Women's organizations?" They thought they might be able to do some good with women's clubs. "There's one other way you can help," I added. "That is, to keep your clients out of this. I think we can win – but only if you keep your clients out."

When it became obvious that the bill would have to be "sold" to the country, FDR himself opened up on the airwaves. On March 14, he plugged his Court scheme in an address to the Democratic party's $100-a-plate "Victory Dinner" at the Mayflower Hotel in Washington. His words were carried over every radio and to 1,100 other such dinners all over the United States. Five days later he pleaded for his bill again in a "fireside chat."

In his dinner speech and in his "fireside chat" the President made a direct appeal to all those groups which could expect to get something from the New Deal if the Court were packed. FDR, impassioned, spoke these now famous words: "Here is one third of a nation ill nourished, ill clad, ill housed . . . if we keep faith with those who had faith in us, if we would make democracy succeed, I say we must act – now!" He pleaded with the people to trust him.

Senator Norris in talking to me said, "You don't trust the President." I replied, "I agreed with Thomas Jefferson who said 'Put your trust in the law rather than man.'" I had heard a good many demagogic speeches, and had undoubtedly made some myself, but I thought this was the most demagogic I had ever heard, and it was coming from the President of the United States!

Replying to the speech, I warned in a radio address: *"Create now a political Court to echo the ideas of the executive and you have created a weapon; a weapon which in the hands of another President could well be the instrument of destruction. A weapon that can cut down those guarantees of liberty written into your great doctrine by the blood of your forefathers and that can extinguish your right of liberty of speech, or thought, or action, or of religion. A weapon whose use is only dictated by the conscience of the wielder."*

Not only did FDR take to the airwaves but all of his cabinet members did likewise.

I had been chosen as the leader of the opposition – I insisted that the networks give us equal time to answer. The networks agreed and I picked out the senators who would answer the administration. Soon, however, I discovered that we were not being given a national audience. For example, a radio debate I had in Chicago with Dean James M. Landis was blacked out everywhere west of the Mississippi except Montana. Officials doubtless figured I would never know the difference. The administration apparently did not want my talk to reach the people west of the Mississippi River.

The President forced into line farm leaders and labor leaders and brought to bear every other pressure he could think of to influence senators in favor of the Court bill. I have never seen such pressure put on legislators. On March 10, the Senate Judiciary Committee opened hearings on S. 1392, "a bill to reorganize the judicial branch of the government." The first witness was Attorney General Homer S. Cummings.

I was scheduled to be the first witness in opposition to the bill. I wanted an opinion from some of the justices so as to start off with a resounding bang for our side, but I knew they would be reluctant to testify on a matter affecting their own integrity. I was trying to figure out some way to get around this problem. Then, on Saturday, March 20, just two days before I was due to appear, I got some encouragement.

Mrs. Brandeis, wife of my good friend, Justice Louis Brandeis, drove over to Alexandria to see my daughter's new baby. When she left she said, "Tell your father I think he is right." I interpreted this as a tipoff that Brandeis was strongly against the bill. I telephoned him for an appointment and went to see him at his apartment. I said I hoped he and the Chief Justice would testify against the charges made by Roosevelt and Cummings that the courts were behind in their work, as well as many other charges. Brandeis said it was his practice not to write or speak publicly about the Court, that all his disagreements were contained in his dissenting opinions. But, the Justice continued, "You call up the Chief Justice and he'll give you a letter?" "I won't call him up,"

I demurred. "I don't know him." "Well, he knows you," Brandeis said.

When I again refused to telephone Hughes, Brandeis called the Chief Justice. He told Hughes I wanted to see him. Hughes suggested I come to his house immediately. The Chief Justice greeted me warmly when I arrived. I told him Brandeis said he would give me a letter. He said, "Did Brandeis tell you that?" I said, "Yes." "When do you want it?" he asked. "Monday morning," I replied. He asked why. "They've circulated a story that I will not testify after all," I explained. "If I put off Monday, they'll say I never will take the stand."

The Chief Justice looked at his watch. "It is now 5:30," he said. "The library is closed, my secretary is gone. I won't have to call Brandeis or Stone and I won't have to call some other justices, but I will have to call some. Can you come by early Monday morning?" "Certainly," I said. Then he asked what I was doing Sunday afternoon. I said "Nothing."

On Sunday afternoon Hughes telephoned my home and asked me to drop by his house. As I walked in, he handed me the letter and said solemnly, "The baby is born." I read the letter and he asked, "Does that answer your question?" "Yes, it does," I said happily. "It certainly does."

I thanked him and started to leave, when he said, "Sit down."

"I think I am as disinterested in this matter—from a political standpoint—as anyone in the United States," the Chief Justice began when we were seated, "because the people of the United States have been far more generous to me than I deserve. I am not interested in who are to be the members of the Court. I am interested in the Court as an institution. And this proposed bill would destroy the Court as an institution."

"If we had an Attorney General in whom the President had confidence," he continued, "and in whom the court had confidence, and in whom the people had confidence, the story might have been different. But the laws have been poorly drafted, the briefs have been badly drawn, and the arguments have been poorly presented. We have had to be not only the Court but we've had to do the work that should have been done by the Attorney General."

I thought to myself, "What a condemnation of Attorney General Cummings."

"You know," Hughes also disclosed, "when Roosevelt was first elected he called me down to the White House and told me he would like to cooperate with the Supreme Court. I said to him, 'Mr. President, the Supreme Court is an independent branch of the government.' He replied that he had always cooperated with the courts in New York and I said, 'Well, that may be, but this is an independent branch of the government.'"

When I left, the Chief Justice said, "I hope you'll see that this gets wide publicity." I almost laughed. "You don't need to worry about that," I assured him.

At 10:30 the next morning I took the stand as the first opposition witness before the Judiciary Committee in the famous marble-walled, ornate caucus room of the Senate Office Building where so many historic hearings have been staged. The room was packed. The chairman of the Committee was the courtly and humorously eloquent Henry Ashurst of Arizona. Senator William H. Dieterich, a Committee member and member of the Kelly-Nash machine in Chicago, was dutifully defending the administration bill. I knew how much he disliked me and so at the start, I said, "I know the Senator from Illinois will not agree with me." I said it again in connection with two other statements about the work of the Court. The third time Dieterich replied, "Of course not." He finally came through with what I wanted.

"Well," I said, "I have a statement from a man who knows more about the Court than the President of the United States, than the Attorney General, than I do, or than does any member of this committee."

Slowly drawing the letter from my inside coat pocket, I continued: "I have a letter by the Chief Justice of the Supreme Court, Mr. Charles Evans Hughes, dated March 21, 1937, written by him and approved by Mr. Justice Brandeis and Mr. Justice Van Devanter."

You could have heard a pin drop in the caucus room while I read the letter aloud. It struck down, one by one, every point raised by Roosevelt and Cummings. The letter concluded ". . . I may also call attention to the provisions of Article III, Section 1, of the Constitution that the judicial power of the United States shall be vested 'in one Supreme Court' and in such inferior courts as the Congress may from time to time ordain and establish. The Constitution does not appear to authorize two or more Supreme Courts functioning in effect as separate courts."

The letter had a sensational effect. The newsreels photographed it, newspaper reporters clamored for copies, and it was all I could do to keep it from being snatched from my hands when the session was recessed. The administration and its supporters were disconcerted by the unexpected counterattack from the eminent leader of the so-called "nine old men."

We heard with amusement that FDR and his strategists were furious at the Chief Justice for "playing politics." The letter put the bill's backers on the defensive. On the morning the debate on the bill was to open in the Senate, I took a phone call from Senator Homer T. Bone, who was in the White House at the time. He asked me if I would come down to see the President. I said, "Certainly," and hung up.

I was at the White House in a few minutes. "Burt, I just want to give you a little background on the Court matter," the President said as I was ushered in. FDR asked me to let the Republicans lead the fight. I told him I had been selected and I would carry on as leader. "Well, let's keep the bitterness out," the President urged. "The Supreme Court and the Constitution are a religion with a great many people in this country," I told him, "and you can't keep bitterness out of a religious fight."

I mentioned that the bill was opposed by Justice Brandeis, who was a liberal before the President and I had ever heard of the word. "Justice Brandeis was all in favor of it, at first," FDR replied wryly, "but the old lady—the nice old lady—kept dropping little drops of water on his head until he changed his mind."

"Whoever told you that was mistaken," I insisted. Mrs. Brandeis dominated the Justice in some ways but I was positive that on questions of law and legislation he certainly made up his own mind.

I told the President that if he dropped the Court bill he could have at least two resignations on the Court. "How can I be sure?" he asked, showing a flicker of interest. "You can be just as sure as Senator Borah and I giving our word," I replied. I had never talked with any of the Justices on this question, but I understood Borah had done so.

Roosevelt insisted that he wanted the bill passed, and I repeated that I was sorry but I couldn't go along with him. We parted without hostility on either side.

I returned to the Senate chamber at noon and found Robinson in his seat waiting to start the debate. "How did you get along down there?" he asked. "Not very well," I replied. "You keep after him, I can't do anything with him," said the majority leader, plainly unhappy about his lieutenant's chore. By the end of May I knew we had an absolute majority of the Senate against the bill.

Senator Robinson was sixty-five years old. He had a quick temper and a heart condition. For many weeks, he had been laboring day and night for the President. As he thundered for the Court bill, he grew pale in the face and Senator Royal S. Copeland of New York, who was a physician, became alarmed and moved over to the seat next to him. "Joe, the cause you're fighting for isn't worth your life!" Copeland whispered. "For God's sake, slow down!" The ordeal proved too much for Robinson. On July 14, five days after I fired the first broadside for us, Robinson was found dead in his apartment.

With Joe Robinson dead, the President's reluctant army was thrown into confusion. Vice-President Garner came to me and asked, "Will you give us two?" Garner meant a compromise that would allow the President to appoint two new Justices instead of six. An erroneous impression had gone around that I would settle for two. It was absurd, because we knew he had the votes to win. "Jack," I said, "I won't give you two, I won't give you one."

"Well, that's out," Garner said philosophically. "What about this idea of a roving judge?" "You don't want a roving judge, Jack," I told him. "If the Department of Justice wanted to convict someone and they had a roving judge they could depend on, they'd send him out to hear the case and he'd hear only one side. Harry Daugherty would have loved to have a roving judge of that kind, and if he had one he would have sent him out to Montana to try me."

"That's out," Garner went on. "What about a proctor?" When I told him he wouldn't want that, he asked me what a proctor was. I said in old English law a proctor was one who managed or administered the handling of cases; that he would be used to go out and check into cases before the court decided to hear them.

"Well," the Vice-President finally said, "go to it and God bless you. Write your own ticket."

Senator Marvel M. Logan of Kentucky, an administration wheelhorse, agreed to move that the Senate send the bill back to the Judiciary Committee. Hiram Johnson rose to make dramatically clear what the recommittal motion signified. "The Supreme Court is out of the way?" he asked. "The Supreme Court is out of the way," Logan responded. "Glory be to God!" exclaimed Johnson. The galleries burst into applause and Garner made no attempt to gavel them into order. And thus ended the fiercest battle in American history between two branches of our government over the third.

In the summer of 1939, speculation over whether FDR would run for a third term was already rife. On August 4, when Congress was preparing to adjourn, I had a long chat with him in the Oval Room of the White House. The court fight was two years past and our relations, despite what most people thought, had become friendly again.

I told him that Senator George Norris, probably his closest friend in the Senate, had come to me recently and said he had a question to ask. Making it clear that he was speaking entirely for himself, Norris had asked, "Would you run for Vice-President with President Roosevelt?" I said my response to Norris was, "No, I wouldn't run for Vice-President with anyone," adding that he should not encourage the President to run in 1940.

I then told FDR that I thought it would be a mistake for him to seek a third term. He immediately interrupted me by saying casually, "Of course, it would be a mistake." The President said, "I don't want to see a reactionary Democrat nominated. I love Jack Garner personally. He is a lovable man, but he couldn't get the Negro vote, and he couldn't get the labor vote."

During the conversation the President said, "Burt, I would like to have you do one thing for me. I'd like to have you make a speech or a statement and say that while you disagreed with me on the method of reforming the Supreme Court, you agreed with me on the objective and that the Court has now been liberalized and that I have won my objective." I was somewhat shocked at how deeply he felt about his defeat. I told him I had made a speech — I think it was in Baltimore — in which I said I had agreed with him that some of the decisions of the Court had been wrong, but that I had disagreed on the way he wanted to correct the situation.

FDR and I then discussed the political situation. He said, "Burt, I think we can win and I want to win in 1940." He added: "we will go along until January,

February, or March. We will get together then. We will sit around and take up different combinations, and try and pick out one that will win."

In the fall of 1939, I raised the question of FDR's intentions while lunching at the Capitol with David K. Niles, the White House assistant in charge of minority groups. "He doesn't want to run and he won't if he can find someone to succeed him who will look upon him as the elder statesman and send him to the peace conference," Niles told me. "Who've you got?" was my next question. "Nobody," said Niles. When I mentioned Senator James F. Brynes of South Carolina, an FDR favorite, Niles replied that Byrnes couldn't be elected because he was an ex-Catholic. When I named Farley, McNutt, and Senate majority leader Barkley, Niles said none of them would do.

Then he said, "You could be elected." I replied that the big city bosses in the party would never stand for me because of my independence. He pointed out that the bosses wanted to win. When I said Roosevelt would never stand for me because I had broken with him on the Court fight, Niles answered: "I've never heard him say anything against you—cross my heart."

One evening in June, 1940, Mrs. Wheeler and I were invited to dinner at the home of Robert E. Kintner, then a columnist partner of Joseph Alsop. The other guests were Leon Henderson, head of the Office of Price Stabilization; Ben Cohen, FDR's able legal draftsman; Edward Foley, general counsel for the Treasury Department, and their wives. After dinner, Henderson leaned back in his chair, removed a big cigar from his mouth, and said, "The convention is going to nominate you for the Vice-President and you're going to have to take it." "No," I said. "Why not?" Henderson asked. "Because the President is going to get us into the war and I won't go out and campaign and say he won't." This was not long after I had been visited by an admiral and an army officer, both of whom warned me that Roosevelt was determined to get us into war.

Henderson said I ought to take the Vice-Presidency under the condition that when the emergency was over, FDR would resign and I would become President. I thought it was a joke. "Will he let me decide 'when the emergency is over'?" I asked, beginning to enjoy myself. At this point, it was pointed out to Mrs. Wheeler – in a typical Washington gambit – that "you'd be the Vice-President's wife." "I'd rather have my husband in the Senate," replied Mrs. Wheeler truthfully.

I never took my candidacy seriously. If FDR didn't choose to run, he could just about name his successor and he must have been irked at my opposition to some of his war policies.

The suspense evaporated on July 9, with the arrival in Chicago of Harry Hopkins, FDR's confidant who lived in the White House, and Senator Byrnes, FDR's right-hand man in the Senate. They were there to stage-manage the President's nomination. Byrnes spent no time in passing the word that the President was available.

The reading of the President's message touched off a pandemonium that could only have been manufactured by the efficient organization of Chicago Mayor Edward J. Kelly. The key instrument – since famous in political annals – was a microphone in the basement of the Chicago Stadium hooked into the loudspeaker system. Pressed close to the microphone was the mouth of Tom Garry, Kelly's Superintendent of Sewers.

"We want Roosevelt!" Garry bellowed, and the amplified words re-echoed around the huge hall like thunderclaps of doom for the avowed candidates. In the galleries as well as on the floor, thousands of the mayor's ward heelers took up the chant. There followed a screaming demonstration for FDR which, under Garry's invisible chant-prompting, continued for fifty-three minutes. To the radio listeners, it must have sounded as if the delegates could not wait until the balloting session to nominate the President. Actually, as has been written elsewhere, the delegates were far from enthusiastic about having traveled all the way to Chicago to be cast in the role of puppets.

Before the convention opened, Moses Cohen, a Los Angeles lawyer originally from my own town of Butte, Montana, had come to my suite in the Congress Hotel. He breathlessly announced that he had just come from a session with Hopkins, Frank Walker, and Edward J. Flynn, the boss from the Bronx. "You can have the nomination for Vice-President," Cohen said. "They're not serious," I assured him. When he insisted that they were serious, I told him I would accept the offer "only if the President calls and asks me." I heard no more from Cohen.

On the opening day of the convention, I had decided to pass up the routine formalities at the Chicago Stadium and take a nap in my suite. I left word that I didn't want to be disturbed. Shortly afterward my son Edward, who was standing guard outside my door, was brushed aside roughly by William H. Hutchinson, the colorful Washington bureau chief of the International News

Service. He barged into my room and told me he had been talking long-distance with Supreme Court Justice Frank Murphy. "Murphy has just left the White House and says that if you will agree to take the Vice-Presidential nomination, the President will call you and ask you to." "I can't do it," I told "Hutch." "He's going to get us into the war and I can't tell people he's going to keep us out." "You are the biggest damn fool in the world!" Hutch exploded. "You'll be the President of the United States if you agree to this."

Four years later I again had lunch with Niles. He again said the President did not want to run but felt he might have to. He did not offer me the Vice-Presidency but he did say that the President would rather have me as a successor than some of those "tories." I told him if I ever had any desire to run for President I didn't any longer, as I felt the man who followed the President might be shot and I didn't want to be a dead hero.

He then asked me about Senator Truman. He said, "Can he make a speech?" I told him he could, though he had not made many in the Senate. He then said, "If the President doesn't run, it will probably be Truman."

Frank Walker, Postmaster General and an old friend of mine from Butte, Montana, called my house one morning and asked me to pick him up on the way to the office. He wanted to discuss the political situation and especially Vice-Presidential candidates. He wanted my opinion of Truman, Byrnes, and Supreme Court Justice William O. Douglas. He wanted to know if I thought the Catholics would fight Byrnes because he had left the Church as a younger man. I told him that he ought to know more about that than I did, since he was a good and prominent Catholic.

Another who came to me with worries about FDR's 1944 running mate was James V. Forrestal, then Secretary of the Navy and privy to many White House matters. At lunch, Forrestal remarked that if Wallace were renominated many influential persons would refuse to support the ticket. He was wondering if Douglas would do.

In September, 1944, Tommy Corcoran was visiting me in my office and we discussed the Democratic convention of that summer. "Why didn't you take the Vice-Presidential nomination?" he asked. "It wasn't offered to me," I replied. "Didn't Dave Niles offer it to you?" Corcoran said. "He was supposed to."

Whether I was ever considered for second place by the President in 1944 I do not know, but I could hardly help feeling that the talks I had with Niles, Walker, and Forrestal were attempts to sound me out on the idea. I liked it down on the floor of the Senate. You can have a real debate there. I also liked the committee work. Altogether, I felt then and I feel now that the office of United States senator is the finest there is—if you are a free man. By this I mean free from dictation by political bosses and control by corporations, labor, or other pressure groups.

A senator as fortunately situated as I was in Montana could disagree with the President even when he was of the same party. To be beholden to any individual or group would have made membership a stultifying experience.

EARL BROWDER

The American Communist Party in the Thirties

Introduction by Herbert Schiller

To the average student entering college today, World War II is ancient history and the period of the thirties is prehistoric. To some of us, that seems a shame for several reasons – not least of which is that in the thirties, we were young. In the United States, the thirties was a period of industrial depression, massive unemployment, and serious discussion of the issue of social reform versus revolution. It was a time of civil rights struggles. It was also a time of fascism on the march, climaxed at the end of the decade by World War II.

Our speaker will, I am sure, touch upon some or all of these episodes. In so doing, he will assist us in understanding some of our current problems and help us recognize that the

Herbert Schiller is research associate professor in the Bureau of Economic and Business Research, University of Illinois.

earlier issues have not really disappeared, but have either been swept under the rug or have assumed new forms.

Earl Browder, head of the American Communist party in the period of its greatest influence, was born in Wichita, Kansas, in 1891. He was the grandson of a circuit-reading Methodist minister from Illinois. His father, a school teacher first in Illinois, then in Kansas, also intended to become a Methodist minister, but he turned Unitarian (under the influence of Emerson). Later, he became a populist and then a socialist. Earl Browder's first venture into active political life occurred when he was fifteen. He and his father joined the Socialist party.

Browder remained in the party only a couple of years, leaving it to join the more radical Syndicalist League of North America which was led by William Z. Foster. Foster, a quarter of a century later, was to succeed Browder as head of the Communist party.

When the Communist party was organized in 1920 from a split within the Socialist party, Browder became one of its charter members. Ten years later he was made general secretary of the party, and for the next fifteen years until the end of World War II he controlled and directed the party's activities.

Under his leadership, the American Communist party attained its greatest influence. Browder was directly responsible for the party's united front activities, which meant cooperation with all groups in American society except those on the extreme left and the extreme right. The party's cry from the mid-thirties on was "Communism is Twentieth Century Americanism." To its list of heroes it added Lincoln and Jefferson, next to Marx and Lenin.

In 1936 and 1940, although a supporter of Roosevelt and the social welfare program of the New Deal, Browder ran for President under the banner of the Communist party. During the brief period of the Hitler-Stalin Pact from August, 1939 until June, 1940, Browder and the party advocated isolationism and sharply criticized Roosevelt's program of Lend Lease and the Selective Services Act. After Hitler attacked the Soviet Union, the party reverted to its earlier position supporting United States involvement against the fascists.

In 1945, after the war, Browder was ousted as head of the Communist party. Since then he has remained outside organized political life.

MY TASK IS TO SHOW HOW and, where possible, why the American Communist party rose in the 1930's to a predominant position among *left* groups and to some national influence.

How unpromising a candidate this party was for such a role. It entered the thirties with a bad record from the twenties. It originated when a majority split-off from the Socialist party in 1919 gave birth not to one but to three parties, each one claiming allegiance to the newly formed Communist International. It took two or three years for the Comintern to secure their unification. Finally, as the Workers party, rid of the leftism of its predecessors, it achieved a working agreement with the Chicago Federation of Labor and its affiliated Farmer-Labor party and from this strong base began a promising growth. But in 1923 all was shattered when the Comintern advised the new party not to join the rising La Follette movement. The Communists violently split with all their new allies. The rest of the twenties was spent in isolation and destructive inner factionalism. The Communist party entered the thirties with a tattered remnant of seven thousand embittered members, a bad reputation as splitters, an unfavorable "public image," and an unknown, untried leadership. The Communists faced a rejuvenated Socialist party on the upswing under Norman Thomas, a leader nationally known and respected among non-Socialists. The outlook was dim, indeed, for the American Communist party as it entered the thirties.

Two new factors were to dominate the thirties, however, and everything depended on how they were faced. The world economic crisis was beginning and Hitler was rising in Germany. It was in meeting these tests that the American Communists began their decade-long spectacular comeback.

The first big steps in that comeback came on March 6, 1930, when vast crowds responded to the call of the Communist party to come out onto the streets and squares to demonstrate for unemployment relief. In the sixty days given to prepare the action the thin network of active Communists and their press would have been totally inadequate to have reached the estimated million persons who responded from coast to coast in the industrial cities of the North. Undoubtedly the majority were informed and attracted by the alarms raised by the daily newspapers, especially the Hearst chain, which saw "Red conspiracies" everywhere. Police Commissioner Whalen, the former floorwalker from Wanamaker's, famous for always having a white gardenia in his buttonhole, became panicky before the sea of faces in Union Square, New York City, and made the day memorable by ordering some bloodletting. Chicago handled the demonstration even more violently. Detroit police did not attack a crowd in Cadillac Square as big as New York's. Overnight by the initiative of the Communists the nation became conscious of the problem of mass unemployment. That day launched the Unemployment

Councils by neighborhood, city, state, and nationally which within a year were recognized by most government institutions dealing with the problem. The National Unemployed Council functioned throughout the thirties until it became the Workers' Alliance to facilitate merger with a smaller rival set up by the Socialists.

It would call for a book to record even a skeleton history of the unemployment movement. But in this brief lecture in which I must at least mention so many things, I can touch on only a few high spots and indicative features of each subject. Thus it is revealing of the nature of the thirties that I was the author of the Unemployment Insurance Bill that was introduced in Congress by Representative Lundeen of Minnesota. Later it was endorsed by the Social Workers Conference, which called all supporting organizations to send delegates to Washington to discuss the bill and lobby for it. This became one of the broadest united front conferences of the decade. I was invited to address the body in recognition of the work of the Communists. Even the Socialist party, which was boycotting conferences that admitted the Communists, sent a delegation headed by Professor Broadus Mitchell (always a united front supporter), and Norman Thomas sent a telegram of support. Congressman Vito Marcantonio, successor to Fiorello LaGuardia, got the bill referred to the Labor Committee, which recommended its passage, the first such action by any committee of Congress. The A.F. of L. was on record opposing unemployment insurance, but after a large number of local unions sent delegates to the Social Workers Conference, President William Green reversed this position and endorsed the rival bill, known as the Wagner-Dingall Bill.

The Wagner Bill was adopted some weeks later, and our bill was left unreported to Congress. We could accept our "defeat" with good grace and even some satisfaction, for the Wagner Bill proved to be an improvement in some ways on the bill sponsored by the left. A bare five years after the campaign for unemployment insurance had begun in earnest with only the Communist and Socialist parties supporting it—and they not cooperating closely—it was already enacted into law. It was an agonizing five years and seemed a long time to the sufferers, but in historical perspective it was extraordinarily quick and easy for such a deep-going reform, the turning point in the evolution of the modern welfare state, as we now appreciate.

Returning to the early thirties, let us take up another "red thread" that runs throughout the decade. With the rise of Hitler to power in Germany, a *Congress Against War* was called in New York City. Under a very broad sponsorship, some 2,500 delegates came, largely from religious organizations, with trade unions as the next largest group. This congress identified Hitler's Germany as the chief source of the danger of war and called for concerted action by the Great Powers to restrain the aggressors before they got too powerful. It launched a continuing organization, the American League Against War and Fascism, with a monthly publication. It held yearly congresses which grew in affiliations until 1939 when it had an affiliated membership of seven million.

The Socialist party, prominent in the first congress along with the Communist party, soon withdrew because of their objection to Communist party participation. The League's first secretary was a Socialist party member, J. B. Matthews, a delegate of the Fellowship of Reconciliation. He resigned after a year, complaining he was not receiving full Communist support. (In 1939 he was to reappear as the anti-Communist expert of the House Un-American Activities Committee.) From that time on the national secretary was an ordained Protestant minister; the one with the longest tenure was Rev. Herman F. Reissig. The solid core of its executive committee from first to last were Roger Baldwin, founder of the American Civil Liberties Union; Dorothy McConnell, daughter of the Methodist Bishop; Margaret Forsythe, of the International Y.W.C.A.; James Waterman Wise, son of Rabbi Stephen S. Wise; and Annie Gray, president of the Women's Peace party. After the first year I was the only Communist member until 1936, when Clarence Hathaway was added, to substitute for me when I was unavailable. Dr. Harry F. Ward, of the Union Theological Seminary, became chairman in 1935 and served until the war. Meta Berger, widow of the first Socialist party congressman from Milwaukee, became a vice-chairman in 1937. These people and people like them on state and city committees made up the solid backbone and directorship of the American League Against War and Fascism (in its last years renamed the American League for Peace and Democracy). It became the center of the crystallization of American public opinion against Hitler-Germany; at the end of the decade the League became so popular that a majority of Roosevelt's cabinet at one time or another became publicly associated with it, either as speakers or sponsors of national or state meetings.

It was only after the war had begun, the League had been dissolved, and the Hitler-Stalin Pact was undergoing its precarious one-and-one-half-year life, that the myth was gradually built up that the League Against War and Fascism was a creation and puppet organization of the Communist party, built on the orders of Stalin. Post mortem, post factum, the League was placed on the Attorney General's well-known list of proscribed organizations as "subversive." No one had made charges against it during its life. It had been ultra-respectable until war came and J. B. Matthews, its first secretary, got to work on its memory through the House Un-American Activities Committee. (In the fifties J. B. Matthews was finally laughed into oblivion when he accused Dwight D. Eisenhower of being a "secret Communist.")

The League was honest, independent, aboveboard, and made no secret of its small but active Communist affiliation. It remains a well-known fact that the Communists here and abroad were pleased that the League helped and registered the turn of American opinion against Hitler, and they supported its activities wholeheartedly. It is also true that by so doing the Communists raised their standing in the American community, even as their rivals of the Socialist party lost proportionately by boycotting the League.

The League operated under the overall slogan: "Keep America Out of War by Keeping War Out of the World." The latter part of the slogan was a warning that if major war came anywhere America would surely be involved but neither League nor Communists advocated American participation except in concerted action with the major powers including Russia. When concerted action was refused by the West, and war came as a result, no agreement remained to bind the League together. The League dissolved, and the Communists reverted temporarily to an isolationist attitude. I was sentenced to prison on an old passport technicality from the days of Herbert Hoover's administration as a consequence of not condemning Stalin's effort at a truce with Hitler. The last days of the thirties found me in jail and on bail, a symbol of the temporary disfavor into which the Communists had fallen.

The struggle for Equal Rights for Negroes was the third field of activity into which the Communists extended their influence. From the early twenties the party made special intensive efforts in this field with little success among Negroes or whites. But in the thirties its work began to stir masses. The first outstanding example was the Angelo Herndon Case. Herndon, a twenty-year-old Negro, went to Atlanta, Georgia, for the Young Communist League to organize Unemployed Councils of Negroes and whites together. He was arrested at the first meeting he called, under a pre–Civil War statute which defined such efforts as sedition. Swiftly tried by an all-white jury, without any chance to prepare a defense, Herndon was convicted, and sentenced to serve twenty years on the chain-gang. The party sent in able northern lawyers, and these enlisted a local Negro as attorney for the defense, Benjamin J. Davis, Jr., son of the Republican party national committeeman of many years standing and a graduate of Harvard. The appeal reached the Supreme Court and was refused a hearing on a technicality. By this time much national interest had been aroused, the churches were being mobilized, the lawyers discovered an issue on which the Supreme Court would review the case which had become "hot" in public attention, and Herndon was freed on bail pending appeal. The Socialist party joined the defense and this was, in my memory, the only united front in which they remained with the Communists until the issue was closed. The final decision of the Supreme Court, which came after Herndon had returned to jail, freed him. The verdict opened a long line of decisions gradually leading up to the historic school integration decision more than two decades later. As one of its significant consequences in the forties, in an election to the New York City Council in which the Republican party elected a single councilman (Stanley Isaacs), Benjamin Davis was elected on the Communist ticket along with Peter Cacchione, and two fellow-travelers on the American Labor party.

The case of the Scottsboro boys, coming after Herndon, dragged out over years, and became world-famous. The Scottsboro boys were a group of young unemployed Negroes, fifteen to twenty-one years of age, beating their way from town to town on freight trains who, camping in the "jungles" near Scottsboro, Alabama, were joined by two white prostitutes also on the road. The camp was raided by deputy sheriffs, and all were arrested. Under the southern code any sexual relations of a Negro male with a white female is rape punishable by death. The Negro boys were all charged with rape, convicted, and sentenced to death. The newspaper, *Daily Worker*, on the initiative of its Communist editor Clarence Hathaway, picked this up from the newswire and launched a protest movement which soon grew to national and then international proportions. This movement was originally organized by the Communists, but after several years, when a group of influential Negro and white church leaders indicated they would take responsibility for the defense if the Communists surrendered all control, the Communists did so when given guarantees that the defense would be energetically pursued. An able attorney, Samuel Liebowitz, undertook the case without fee, and after securing reversal of the death sentence and a retrial, he conducted a sensational defense that put the South on trial before the whole world. Eventually most of the boys were freed after years, but some died in prison, victims of provocation. Samuel Liebowitz became a judge, probably as a direct result of the fame arising from this defense, and left a distinguished legal record. He took up the case after the Communists had focused world attention upon it. During this campaign Communist speakers had free entry to the pulpits of most Negro churches.

The National Negro Congress began at the height of public interest in the Scottsboro case as an autonomous attempt to unify the Negro community and make it a political force. The call for its formative congress was signed by a representative cross section of Negro leaders of all political groups, including Socialists and Communists. At its first meeting this was taken for granted; there was no controversy about my appearance on the panel of speakers. Afterward, however, the Socialist party raised objection to the inclusion of Communists, and Socialist members Randolph and Crossthwaite resigned from its executive committee. The main body under its secretary, John P. Davis, stood firm on its original position and continued throughout the thirties. Davis was an active Democratic party worker, but he welcomed the participation of the Communists in his organization until the middle forties.

It should be noted that the American Communist party made few converts to Communism among the

Negroes; its influence was based solely on its militancy and consistency in the struggle for equal rights.

In passing I must mention one of the Communists' mistakes on the Negro question, namely, the issuance of the slogan "self-determination for the Black Belt." The Negro masses were completely indifferent to it, and the Communists soon quietly shelved it. An attempt was made to revive it during the leftist hysteria that gripped the party after 1945, but even the extreme Fosterites finally had to drop it as utterly unrealistic.

The American Youth Congress was a fourth major point of concentration for the Communist leadership, and particularly for the activity of young Communists, during the thirties. It eventually was the field of some of the most successful united front work, although the Communists had nothing whatever to do with originating it. Its founder was a young woman named Viola Ilma, who was sponsored by Eleanor Roosevelt and Anne Morgan. After spending a few years in the stirring youth movement of Europe, including some time in Spain and Germany under the extreme right, Ilma returned to America with visions of a mass youth movement which she would lead. Her call for a mass youth congress in 1934, with money for advertising and the prestige of her sponsorship, gained a broad response especially among the church-youth organizations, even including Catholic ones, as well as what she considered the "negligible" left organizations. But when the delegates assembled at the First American Youth Congress, Ilma so far forgot her American background as to announce herself as permanent chairman without the formality of election. The body of church delegates objected to this and turned to the more sophisticated although "negligible" left for leadership of their revolt. The Socialist and Communist youth forgot their differences and immediately united to provide that leadership. From that moment they remained united, and dominated and Youth Congress throughout the thirties, until, with the onset of war, it rapidly dissolved. As an example of how important and valued their forum became in national politics we may note that when Robert Taft made his bid for the Senate, his campaign manager asked the American Youth Congress to grant him their platform in their congress scheduled for Cleveland. The youth leaders replied they would gladly do so, provided he made his appearance as one of the political panel already invited, which included myself for the Communist party. The Tafts agreed, and Robert Taft sat smilingly on the platform along with myself, and the picture was printed in the newspapers without arousing any comment. It was a decade later, in the era of Senator Joe McCarthy, that a similar but *faked* photo was sufficient to purge Senator Millard Tydings. In the thirties it *helped* get elected to the Senate the man who was to become "Mr. Republican himself."

Closely related to the Youth Congress movement but having their own distinct development were the student organizations led by the socialists and communists respectively, and their unification before the end of the decade. Their origin goes back before the First World War to the Intercollegiate Socialist Society founded by Upton Sinclair and Harry Laidler, and their first splits follow the lines of the party split, roughly speaking. Their activities moved onto a broader field after the rise of Hitler and the threat of the Second World War. The first stirring of the new era began around the Oxford

Pledge movement ("I will not fight for King or country") and the Strike Against War which became international in the early thirties. In America it rapidly threw off its pacifist tinge to become directly anti-Hitler, and to demand concerted action of the western democracies to halt Hitler. Symptomatic of this change was that at Brooklyn College, where the strike showed almost complete involvement of the student body. The united committee heading it invited me as one of the main speakers to address the strikers on the campus. I was already being recognized as a leading spokesman of American involvement in a stop-Hitler coalition. By the latter thirties the *New Republic*, liberal weekly, chose the historian Charles Beard and myself to represent the two sides of the national issue of the day: isolationism versus concerted action against Hitler.

The life of the rapidly growing student organizations revolved around the proposal, backed by the Communist party and opposed by the Socialist party, for their merger into a united American Student Union. The Socialist party opposed the merger so bitterly that when the majority of Socialist students approved the merger, the Socialist party expelled Joe Lash and others from the party for carrying out the mandate of their membership. The Socialist party thus isolated itself from the united organization, as they did on the same issue from the unemployed organization.

The fifth field of activity on which I focus attention is the rise of the left in the trade unions, although it was first in our allocation of forces, and was basic to all our other work. But the pattern of trade union development was very complex and it is more difficult to summarize. There were more changes in the main tactical line. The thirties opened with the Communists emphasizing independent trade unions, and for a while an independent center, the Trade Union Unity League. By 1934, some of these unions had stabilized themselves and gained such strength that they were invited to rejoin the American Federation of Labor (A.F. of L.), from which they had been expelled in the twenties, and where favorable terms could be negotiated, they did so. Then the less sturdy ones were dissolved. Shortly afterward the Committee for Industrial Organizations was formed within the A.F. of L., and when that was expelled and the Committee turned into a Congress, the Communist-influenced unions went with it. The C.I.O. then began mass organizing in the steel, auto, electrical, marine, transport, and other fields where the Communists already had established significant toeholds.

In the twenties John L. Lewis, president of the Miners Union, had been the chief enemy of the Communists and had purged them from the industry. This served the double purpose of eliminating his opposition in the union, and carrying out his pact with the mine owners to reduce the labor force and introduce machine mining. The uprooted miners poured into the growing automobile industry, thus furnishing the main body of the first recruits to the leftist auto union which was the nucleus of the future United Auto Union under the C.I.O. In addition to these assets on the side of the Communists, about one-third or one-quarter of the party membership were more or less experienced union organizers trained in a tough school when organizing was a kind of guerilla warfare. John L. Lewis had carried on a running battle with their kind in mining for over ten years and had a keen personal appreciation of their qualities. Therefore when he launched the C.I.O. mass campaigns he invited the Communists to join his staff (second only to his personal machine from the miners' union).

Thus with the rise of the C.I.O. the Communists rose with it as a trade union power. Lewis, the nemesis of the Communists in the twenties, was transformed into their patron saint in the thirties—except in mining where they were still rigidly excluded. By the close of the decade the Communists and their closest allies had predominant influence in unions representing approximately one-third of the membership, and various degrees of minority influence in another third. Added to this was their "understanding" with the centrist leadership to complete the isolation of the open anti-Communists. By the forties some students of the labor scene had already raised the question: "Who is using whom, Lewis or the Communists?"

That question received an answer of a kind in 1941. Lewis disappeared from the C.I.O., but the Communists remained. This is a story that properly belongs to the forties, but since its foundation was laid in the thirties it must at least be mentioned here. The Communists were a growing influence in the C.I.O. until 1945; their subsequent downfall was entirely of their own doing. On the pattern of 1923 the Communists followed the suggestion of the Russians, turned their backs on their own best judgment, split with their closest allies with bitterness and recriminations, and headed into political oblivion with enthusiasm. After 1945, however, the American Communist party was to have no second chance. The welfare state had cut the ground out from under it. Let us go back to the thirties.

The rise of the C.I.O. trade unions carried the whole

labor movement with it. It was the basis of the Communist advances in all other fields. We have given here only a few points of orientation to bring the details into focus. The existing literature on it is so fragmentary, so full of special pleading, so cluttered with myths and legends with no serious factual basis, as to be almost worthless for an understanding of history, or worse than useless. One is sorely tempted to enlarge on the subject, but limitation of time pulls one up sharply. In one single lecture, I must indicate the broad field covered by Communist advances in the thirties. If I speak mainly of the positive side of their work, it is because I have undertaken to explain the unexpected *rise* of the Communists, not the story of their *fall*, which belongs to the latter half of the forties and which resulted from a sharp turnabout in policy, and to which only the 1923 debacle bears any resemblance.

The U.S. presidential election of 1936 began to cast its shadow by the opening of 1935. A complex regrouping of forces was beginning; labor unions were rising under the stimulus of Section 7(a) of the National Recovery Act which at last made collective bargaining a legal right (the only lasting change introduced by the N.R.A.); the San Francisco General Strike had taken place with a settlement favorable to labor; General Hugh ("Ironpants") Johnson, then regarded as pro-fascist, was out of the Roosevelt cabinet; Al Smith had launched his Liberty League offensive with allies in the administration as well as the Republicans. It was a time for redetermination of friends and enemies for everyone. The New Deal had crystallized in its historic meaning.

I must deal with these developments as I saw them in my post as head of the American Communist party, because that party followed my lead unanimously for over the next decade. I can assume that my thinking dominated it and its allies whether or not they all shared my thought in detail.

By 1935 the Communist party had immensely improved its situation; it was participating in rapidly growing mass organizations; it had increased its own membership fourfold; the independent unions it led were being invited back into the A.F. of L. under favorable terms; it had won "citizenship" in the labor movement. It still had the unfavorable public image inherited from the twenties, but when Floyd Olson, the Farmer-Labor governor of Minnesota, called a nationwide conference of significant leaders of the "Left" to meet in Chicago, he sent me a personal invitation. It was agreed that state labor parties and the unions would endorse Roosevelt for a second term, but all that was desired from the Communists was that they place no obstacles in the way and that they consult on new issues as they arose. Our relations with Olson were already those of close cooperation, and thereafter they improved with the unions, notably the Amalgamated Clothing Workers (Hillman), from whom we had been estranged since the debacle of 1923–24.

Some months thereafter I headed a delegation to Moscow to consult with the Comintern about the elections. Upon arriving we were informed by Georgi Dmitrov, the Bulgarian who had become General Secretary at the Seventh World Congress and the hero of the Reichstag Fire Trial in Nazi Germany, that the Comintern leaders were all firmly of the opinion that the American Communist party should endorse Roosevelt's candidacy and put up no candidate of their own. My permanent (but usually secret) opposition in America, William Z. Foster (supported by Sam Darcy) immediately agreed with the proposal. I flatly opposed it, and proposed a thorough discussion before decision, the rest of the delegation withholding their opinion. After two weeks of discussion I remained obdurate, and advanced my final argument that if we really wished to assure Roosevelt's re-election we would not endorse him because that would cause him to be labeled "the Communist candidate" by the newspapers, most of which opposed him. This would lose him many times as many votes from the "Right" as it would bring him from the "Left," for a net loss that might mean his defeat if the vote were close. On the other hand we could put up our own candidate but conduct such a campaign that would assure Roosevelt all votes under our influence except the diehard opponents of all "capitalist" candidates who without a Communist condidate would switch to Norman Thomas or even the Socialist Labor party. Thereupon the discussion was suspended, while the issue was being re-evaluated by the Russian Polburo—which we learned later meant by Stalin. The final conclusion of the Comintern was "to leave the matter to the decision of the American comrades," where I had no difficulty in carrying the decision my way. Thus I became the logical Communist presidential candidate and made my ambiguous campaign in favor of "my rival," Roosevelt. The more the newspapers puzzled over this tactic, the more effective it became.

The Spanish Civil War and the Abraham Lincoln Battalion requires an important place in any evaluation of the thirties. Some two thousand Americans enlisted in the Spanish Republican Army to fight the mutiny of General Francisco Franco and his Moorish cohorts with their Nazi and fascist auxiliaries; more than half of these volunteers died on Spanish battlefields. They fought in a special unit, the Abraham Lincoln Battalion, a name emphasizing the political aim to preserve the republic, not to turn the war into a socialist revolution. I was its chief organizer and gave it its name. I was an invited guest at the last meeting of the republican legislature that met near Barcelona at Montserrat, and visited the front at Teruel where the Americans fought in one of the most bloody battles of the war. By that time the Americans and Canadians, despite their heavy losses, were the largest single contingent in the International Brigade recruited from all over Europe.

This was the only point in my life when I was openly and flagrantly acting in defiance of an American law—namely the Neutrality Act which was passed for the specific purpose of keeping Americans from acting to support the Spanish Republic on the theory that this would "keep America out of war." Most of my adult life from 1917 to 1955 was spent under one or another indictment for alleged violations, but for this instance when I was clearly "guilty" I was never even officially questioned, not to mention indicted. When some doctors in Detroit, who at my request had given the volunteers their physical examination before they went to Spain, were indicted for their action, the ensuing storm of public indignation was great enough to cause Washington to quash the indictments promptly. No official wanted to test how deep American sympathy was for the beleaguered Spanish Republic. The American Communists shared in that public sympathy.

2

In the first part I have set forth a bare skeleton of fact with a minimum of analysis. Choosing facts which I consider significant for evaluating the thirties implies some theory. Perhaps I should state it explicitly. Briefly, it is that in the study of history more light is shed by dealing with the *consequences* of an action. We find that when we search for *motives*, their importance becomes distorted with the lapse of time. A corollary is that the historical significance of action is seldom if ever known to the actors at the time, but is only *discovered* afterwards by historical research and analysis.

The New Deal, with its inadequacies and mistakes (it was stingy in its social expenditures – even the Eisenhower interim was almost munificent by comparison – and its limitation of production represented an economic blind-alley) had put America on the road to the welfare state and thereby had cut the ground from under both the Socialist and Communist parties – yet it certainly had the enthusiastic support of the latter. No mass discontent with the economic system existed except such as provides the basis for *reform* movements. The traditionally reformist Socialist party reached the mistaken conclusion that the movement of more and more of its following toward the Communist party resulted from the attraction of its revolutionary talk. This led the Socialist party to use revolutionary phrases; witness the platform it adopted in the Detroit Convention. At the same time the Socialist party thought the New Deal had pre-empted the whole field of reform. The immediate consequence was a series of splits (the Social-Democratic Federation centered around *The New Leader* in New York, the Connecticut socialists led by Mayor Jasper McLevy of

Bridgeport, the Milwaukee socialists under Mayor Dan Hoan), leaving them weaker than before. Thereafter the Socialist party declined in influence from year to year, never able to decide whether it was reformist or revolutionary, and constantly falling between two stools.

The Communist party, on the other hand, rapidly moved out of its extreme leftist sectarianism of 1930 toward the broadest united front tactics of reformism for strictly limited immediate aims. It relegated its revolutionary socialist goals to the ritual of chapel and Sundays on the pattern long followed by the Christian Church. On weekdays it became the most single-minded practical reformist party that America ever produced. Thus the Socialist party, despite its initial advantages over the Communists, lost ground steadily to them. By the middle of the thirties the positions of the two parties were reversed, the Communists had the upper hand in all circles that considered themselves left of the New Deal.

This does not mean that throughout the thirties the Socialist party did not retain the adherence of many of the ablest "men of the left"—among the many such an outstanding example was Powers Hapgood. It was that the Socialist party wasted most of this potential capital; never welded them into a coherent group, never gave them a common policy that would make them more than individuals, and gave them little voice in the party leadership.

Norman Thomas was given formal adherence as national leader; his personal influence was wider than that of his party. But the practical leadership was in the hands of the factions which ignored him, tried to reduce him to a decorative figurehead, useful mainly for public relations. Like all factional leaderships that of the Socialist party was less and less united, less and less capable of formulating or following a consistent policy. Nor were they able to learn from either their own successes or failures. They learned nothing, for example, from their successful continental congress in the early thirties, nor from the spectacular capture of the Democratic party primary in California by Upton Sinclair's EPIC movement ("End Poverty In California"). Nor did they learn from their failure to halt the Communist advance by boycotting the unity movements (in the unemployed organizations, the American League Against War and Fascism, the National Negro Congress, and among the students). They repeated all their failures but none of their successes. It was left to the Communists to learn from their successes; e.g., they copied Sinclair's EPIC movement and largely absorbed its remains when Sinclair retired from politics.

In contrast to the growing disarray in the Socialist leadership, the Communist party which in the twenties had given the extreme example of inner struggles, united with increasing solidarity until 1945. I had become secretary in 1930 and by April of 1934 (Cleveland convention) had become the unquestioned leader for the next eleven years. If factions persisted they had to keep secret and did not seriously disturb the party life; my policies were adopted unanimously after free discussion at each convention. In 1936 I became a public as well as a party figure. For the last half of the 1930's the Communist party regularly filled the biggest halls from coast to coast (except in the South) for my public appearances.

The influence of the Communist International (Comintern) upon the American Communist party impinges upon my theme crucially, and in many ways. Forgive me if I extend myself beyond the decade to sketch its background.

The Comintern was the child of the Russian Revolution and, in a special sense, of Lenin. It was a deliberate planned split of the Labor and Socialist (Second) International, which traced its ancestry back to Marx and Engels on one side, and Ferdinand Lasalle, founder of the German Social-Democratic party, on the other.

It was a split over the *timing* of the common aim of world socialist revolution. The Communist and Socialist parties that resulted were as hostile as two estranged brothers. They might be likened to two devoutly Christian brothers split over when to prepare for the Second Advent of Christ, one saying He is coming in the immediate future, the other saying no, not for twenty years yet! Lenin said the world revolution was beginning, and the Russian Revolution was only its first adumbration. Lenin died in 1924. More than a decade passed without a major revolution; the date of the world revolution was postponed from year to year. But Lenin's dogma was frozen in the Comintern, for no successor had the authority or prestige to change it. The very idea of change became the great heresy, *revisionism.* The world revolution as the inspiration of Communism survived all disappointments as to its date and even the dissolution of the Comintern during the war to bolster Russia's alliances (as epochal as though Christians dissolved their Church). After the Second World War the breakup of outdated empires and Russia's new eminence as a world power bolstered the fading vision of world socialist revolution and gave it a new substitute acceptable to the truly faithful. The Socialist party forgot its ancient goal of world revolution.

Lenin had established an internal regime in the Comintern that was a complex of tensions. First there was the tension between the split with the Second International which remained basic, on one side, and the tempering of the split with "partial" united fronts for immediate non-socialist aims, on the other side. Second, there was the tension between the ascendency of the Russian party in world Communism, on one hand, and gestures toward equality of parties recognized in principles. The contradiction was "reconciled" in the phrase "First among equals" to fix the Russian position, but the emphasis subtly shifted back and forth between "first" and "equals" as policy shifted. In the first half of the decade, the emphasis was on the split and on Russian primacy in the Comintern; in the second half of the thirties as the menace of Hitler grew, the emphasis shifted back to "united front" and the equality of parties.

In brief, the Comintern policy was a shifting mixture of dogma and response to pressures. Of the latter, I cite the initiative of the French party early in 1935 for the "Front Populaire," and as mentioned before my own ability to change Comintern decisions. Students of the thirties who assume the "Comintern line" was a fixed, homogenous thing will miss the essence of the period, which was change. In the last months of 1939 the "line" disappeared entirely.

The role of the USSR in world politics, aside from all angles of the "Comintern questions," had a shifting significance in America. For the American Communist party in 1930 the USSR began as something to be "defended" against a world *hostile to it*; by 1936 the USSR was being increasingly transformed into a potential *ally* of America as part of the concerted defense of both countries against rising fascist powers *hostile to both.* Then for the first time the agitation of the American Communist party began to get a *response in depth* when it spoke of the USSR; the special relationship of the Communists to the USSR for the first time became a political asset to the party instead of a net liability. Practically the whole anti-Hitler movement, organized in the American League Against War and Fascism, adopted the Communists' view on this question; this probably was the chief reason why the Socialist party boycotted the League.

The outbreak of the Second World War, although long threatened, was a series of shocking surprises to most people, not least to myself. I was invited in the summer of 1939 to speak at the summer Institute of Politics at the University of Virginia, Charlottesville, and was provided with accommodations for myself and my wife for the week of the Institute. Among the other speakers there I found my friend Louis Fischer and Norman Thomas; the others I did not know personally. Present were about forty military men, who followed the speakers on the international situation quite keenly. One of them asked me the Communist opinion of what Stalin would do if not given the alliance he would seek from the British-French mission soon to be in Moscow. I replied that failure to complete the British-French-Russian alliance in the forthcoming negotiations was "unthinkable," and I refused to speculate on an alternative. My questioner then referred to Stalin's recent speech at the Russian Party Congress as a sign that to Stalin it was not "unthinkable," and wanted my opinion whether in that event Stalin would turn to an alliance with Hitler. I replied that I could easier imagine myself being elected president of the U.S. Chamber of Commerce. That brought a laugh that ended the questions.

It was only some weeks later that the failure of the British-French mission in Moscow became clear. The mission had not even been authorized to discuss a treaty with Moscow. It was the British and French governments to whom the alliance itself had been "unthinkable." The alternative Stalin chose was "neutrality" — already the declared policy of America — a Russian counterpart of American isolationism. He signed the Ribbentrop-Molotov Pact.

Britain's failure to even discuss a war treaty with Russia was, to me, surprising and shocking. Apparently to the American press, or its most articulate section at least, what was surprising and shocking was that Stalin should emulate American isolation instead of engaging Germany at war single-handedly. Indignation was not directed at Chamberlain for making the alliance with Russia impossible, but at Stalin for refusing to act as ally despite Chamberlain kicking him in the face. To read the American newspapers of the day, one would believe "Stalin Launches World War." In later years I have come to believe many atrocious stories about Stalin, but never that one. It was a moment of hysterical unreason for the American press and those responsive to it.

I had a personal glimpse of our press at its worst at that moment. In the country on a few days rest, I received the information on the telephone that a pact had been signed between Hitler and Stalin, and the newspapers were demanding interviews with me. I had no authentic information whatever, but I agreed to meet the press next morning in my office since the alternative was to see headlines: "BROWDER IN HIDING." When I walked into my office the next morning it was packed with reporters and photographers. A mob scene followed as each reporter tried to get his question in first, and photographers trod on each other. One might imagine that it was I making decisions of war or peace. When order was restored it became clear that all questions were hostile to the Soviet Union, and were, in effect, demanding that I condemn Stalin's action. One question I could answer: No, I had received no information about the Pact other than the news releases, and these told nothing of the details. It was not my place to judge the wisdom or otherwise of Stalin's decisions. But whatever his action, it had come *after* he had offered an alliance to Britain and France which had not been accepted (I did not yet know it had not even been discussed). No, I would say no word in condemnation or criticism of Stalin. The press had what it wanted, and rushed to get into print; "Browder Supports Pact Which Starts World War" was a typical headline.

I knew, of course, that the reporters had orders, spoken or implicit, from their editors, as to the kind of story that was to emerge from that interview. What surprised me was the reporters' display of emotion. They were angry at me, they held me responsible for Stalin who had gone against their wishes.

I went from the hostile interview to an equally puzzling luncheon with Granville Hicks, literary editor of the *New Masses* weekly. Hicks was not hostile. He implored me — the word is apt — to tell him something that would make sense of the Hitler-Stalin Pact. "It is just as shocking to me as to you," I told him. "I could not conceive that London and Paris would refuse Moscow that alliance which was Stalin's price for mobilization against Hitler. But when it was refused, what did you expect Stalin to do?" Hicks replied: "We could all *die* with honor." It was clear that Hicks was leaving us. I made no further attempt to dissuade him; his advice to die with honor seemed to me a bit inadequate except for the saving of souls. He never should have joined *any* political party. I could not have a hard feeling toward him. The harshest word I had for him was my general remark that stormy winds carry off the dry leaves first. Hicks represented a type of sensitive intellectual unfitted for the harsh realities of political decisions in war. But only years later could I trace the pattern which the type represented by Hicks followed in all countries.

The split of a few hundred intellectuals like Hicks did not weaken the party, for their places were taken by ten times as many trade unionists, who were basically isolationists themselves and admired Stalin for "turning isolationist" and the American Communists for their practical qualities. But our temporary unpopularity was serious for me personally, for it enabled my political enemies to load me with a prison sentence for a passport technicality, which outraged even Wendell Willkie, the Republican presidential candidate in 1940.

There had grown in the late thirties, as a part of the pro-Soviet and anti-Hitler sentiment generally, an extreme idealization of the USSR among certain intellectual circles as the "one hope" of the world. When Stalin signed a *neutrality* pact with Hitler their world collapsed, he betrayed their dream of a kindly Providence saving the reckless and improvident nations. They were more bitter against Stalin than against Hitler, if that were possible, for Hitler was only making good his threats while Stalin had *withdrawn* his protecting hand. In the best interpretation Stalin had run from the battle, and in the worst he had joined the enemy. As Granville Hicks indicated to me, such men expected Stalin to fight alone, and if he could not conquer, at least to "die with honor." They demanded a miracle and their God failed them.

Appropriately enough the title, *The God That Failed,* was the name an international group gave their collection of essays written later, to explain why they broke with Communism over the issue of the Hitler-Stalin Pact. I do not criticize them for breaking with Communism; I only point out the inadequacy of their explanation and the inappropriateness of the moment chosen. For one and all of these idealists rallied round Roosevelt whose "neutrality" furnished Stalin with his model, and which dissolved into war at the moment Hitler chose, just as Stalin's did. It took Hitler's aggression to forge the Grand Alliance required to stop him. Until the war broke out in 1939, Stalin's crimes were primarily against the Russian people, or those classified as such by American governments since Wilson. His international crimes came later.

In dealing with history I have no special cause to defend. It may be suspected that I wish to prove my own correctness in the past. But I am quite indifferent to that aspect. Correct or incorrect, however, I do wish events to be objectively set forth. Then they can speak for themselves. I hate historical distortions, whatever their source. It is in this spirit I would say a few more words about my prison sentence: when my appeal came to the Supreme Court, the prosecution found it necessary to reduce the alleged offense to a mere technicality (*malum prohibitum not malum in se* was the legal phrase); and after I had gone to prison President Roosevelt commuted the sentence *in wartime* as a contribution "to national unity." Apparently my prosecution had weakened America in the war.

3

The American Communist party, entering the 1930's as an ultra-leftist political sect of orthodox Marxist-Leninist ideology, found itself engaged in practical struggles for immediate aims, among which special importance was given to social insurance and a strong trade union movement. By 1935 social insurance was established in principle and a big upsurge in trade unionism was underway. By participating in these struggles the Communist party had strengthened itself; its influence in the nation was no longer negligible. These activities were essentially *reformist*. As a *revolutionary* party it had not advanced an inch. On the contrary it had buttressed the Roosevelt New Deal and postponed revolutionary prospects indefinitely. Without a revolutionary situation a revolutionary party either stagnates in isolation, or it finds itself engaged in struggles which are reformist. Then it either becomes *consciously* reformist, or, as in the case of the American Communists, divorces orthodox theory from practice, and, as we noted before, follows the model of the early Christian Church, and saves the theory for Saints' Days Celebrations.

From the other side of the world, and from an opposite pole of social-economic development, the Communist party of China was having an analogous contradiction between Marxist-Leninist dogma and the real world. True, China had a permanent revolutionary situation, but the class structure of her society refused to fit into the dogma. The Chinese Communist party had recurring friction with its Russian "elder brother" and chafed under its tutelage. Mao Tse-tung came to the leadership of the party out of the collapse of its Russian-supported leadership and the simultaneous lightening of Comintern centralism in the mid-thirties. He was contemptuous of dogma, and was widely quoted as saying: "It is not worth as much as cow-dung, which is at least useful for fertilizer." Because he flouted so many Comintern dogmas, and became head of the party without Russian support, Mao was associated with the revisionist trend in the Comintern, both by reputation and by actual collaboration. But similar to the American Communist party, the Chinese party remained "orthodox" in theory, "reinterpreting" theory to conform to their new practice as it became necessary.

It was against this background that I particularly welcomed a series of letters in 1937 from the leaders of the Chinese Communist party. My friend Philip Jaffe, editor of the monthly, *Amerasia,* accompanied by his wife Agnes, visited Yennan that summer and transmitted my greetings to the leaders there. In response Mao Tse-tung, Chou En-lai, and Chu Teh, the three principal leaders at that time, wrote me letters on June 24, which Jaffe brought back to me. They were published at the time. In the light of subsequent events they take on added historical interest, which may justify quoting them here. The letter from Mao Tse-tung read:

My dear Comrade Browder:

Taking advantage of comrade's visit, I am sending this letter to you, our respected Comrade Browder, good friend of the Chinese people and leader of the American people.

Both the Communist party of China and the Communist

party of U.S.A. are confronted with a historic task, the task of resisting and overthrowing the aggressive policy of Japanese imperialism. The Chinese party is endeavoring to bring about an anti-Japanese national united front. Although our work is passing through a difficult period, we have already made progress and we are doing our best to bring about the desired result.

From several American friends, and from other sources, we have learned that the Communist party of the United States and the masses of the American people are deeply concerned with China's struggle against Japan and have given us assistance in many ways. This makes us feel that our struggle is by no means isolated and we are heroically assisted from abroad. At the same time we feel that when we achieve victory, this victory will be of considerable help to the struggle of the American people for liberation. The world is now on the eve of a great explosion. The working class of the world and all the peoples who desire liberation must unite for the common struggle.

Revolutionary Greetings,
Mao Tse-tung

The second letter, from Chou En-lai, of the same date read:

Comrade Browder:

From the comrade who visited us we learned what concern you and the Communist party of the United States have for the Chinese revolutionary movement and what enthusiastic assistance you have given us. This news gives us great stimulation.

Comrade, do you still remember the Chinese comrades who worked with you in China ten years ago? I am among those who made your acquaintance at that time. Unfortunately Comrade Su Chao-chen, whom you knew best, is no more with us. He died of sickness in 1929, when he was working under the most difficult conditions.

After the Sian incident, the Chinese Communist party and the Kuomintang have again started negotiations. We are dealing with a new problem of the united front which is not exactly like the united front negotiations between the Communists and Socialists in Europe and America. It is also different from the kind of cooperation which we had with the Kuomintang between 1924 and 1927. The objective of the united front at the present time is to fight Japanese imperialism. Thus, in China at the present time, the concrete process of bringing about the united front and the content of the united front is very devious and complicated. As to what actually happened and what is the present status of the negotiations I have already transmitted this to you.

I fervently hope that you and the party under your leadership will give us more support. I am also anxious to get your opinion on our united front work. I am confident that with our two parties on both sides of the Pacific working to overthrow the devil of aggression in the Pacific and later to overthrow all aggressors, we will surely succeed.

Enthusiastic Bolshevik greetings to you.

Chou En-lai

The third letter is from the commander of the Red Army. He wrote:

On behalf of the Chinese People's Army, I am sending to you and through you to the Communist party of the United States, the American workers and farmers and all American friends of the Chinese national liberation movement our enthusiastic greetings.

We are determined to exert our utmost to unite the Chinese people for the purpose of driving out Japanese imperialist bandits and struggle for the freedom and liberation of China. In this struggle we hope you will give a great deal of fraternal assistance. Let us join hands and destroy the dark and barbaric system of fascism. Our future is bright and is bound to be illuminated by the progress that is bound to shine in both hemispheres.

Long live the solidarity of the Chinese and the American people!

Long live the victory of our struggle against fascism!

Chu Teh

I quote these letters in full to establish the historical fact that the Chinese leadership, the same group essentially that today heads the Communist Republic of China, approved my policies in 1937; they valued my support and emphasized their feelings by writing *three* simultaneous personal letters by the three chief leaders. More than a quarter-century later they rewrote history to justify their split with the Russians and to make me the original modern "revisionist." In 1964, in the VIII installment of "The Open Letter" polemic with the Russians, by the editorial departments of *Renmin Ribao* (*People's Daily*) and *Honggi* (*Red Flag*), they summed up their new history with the following passages; "an adverse current of revisionism was chiefly represented by Browder, later by Tito, and now by Khrushchev. Browder began to reveal his revisionism around 1935."[1]

Around 1935 is the period when I began to feel the influence of Mao Tse-tung. He was the first successful revisionist of Comintern doctrine I knew. The Peking chronology of revisionist leaders should therefore give Mao priority. The list should read; Mao Tse-tung, Browder, Tito, Khrushchev. It was only in the fifties that Mao revised his revisionism to become ultra-leftist. I knew him as part of the right wing, to which I belonged, and Tito as part of the extreme left wing, which he rapidly changed to right wing only after he was expelled from the Cominform. At any rate Mao thought highly of me in 1937.

He continued to think highly of me *eight years later* in 1945, as I approached the end of my leadership of American communism. At the foundation meeting of the

[1] "The Proletarian Revolution and Khrushchev's Revisionism," *Foreign Languages Press* (Peking, 1964), p. 51.

United Nations at San Francisco, the Chinese Government, headed by Chiang Kai-shek, named as one of its delegates a prominent Communist, Tung Pi-wu, whom I knew from my 1927 sojourn in China. The Chinese Communists undoubtedly knew this was the result of a suggestion from Franklin Delano Roosevelt, and they must have suspected it was inspired by my influence. However that may be, Tung arrived in New York first, without coming through Russia. He met me and in full confidence gave me a secret cipher of confidential communications with Mao. From New York, he went to San Francisco where he met the Russian delegation. When he returned to New York he refused to meet me. He had since been informed of my coming purge.

The Chinese party had no choice but to follow the Russian lead in denunciation of me as a "revisionist." When Foster took over the leadership of the American party a few weeks later, Mao sent him a telegram of congratulations. This was published in the *Daily Worker*—but with deletions. Among the deletions were the words in which Mao, at the moment he was parting company with me under Russian orders, went out of his way to state his high opinion of me in terms he had never used before. He said: *"In his past activity, Comrade Browder has rendered many services to the struggle of the Chinese people, which deserve our gratitude."*[2]

It belongs in a general history, or especially that of the forties, to explain the "many services" I had rendered the Chinese Communist party in the period 1927–45 when I had close relations with its leaders.

[2] Stuart R. Schram, "The Political Thought of Mao Tse-tung," *Chiang-fang Jihpao*, July 31, 1945 (New York and London: Praeger, 1963).

This much of an excursion outside the thirties period was required to establish that the "new history" of the Chinese party, which dates my "revisionism" from 1935, has nothing whatever to do with what they thought and felt about me until 1945. Whether their later enlightenment in the sixties is a self-correction in the light of "deeper wisdom" or whether it is political opportunism, each student must judge for himself.

My outline of significant points in the history of the American Communist party in the thirties should end here. Many interesting features have been entirely omitted because they do not lend themselves to a brief summing up, or because they are only marginally related to the rise of Communist influence to *national* significance (e.g., on both counts, the considerable impact of the Communist party on the cultural and intellectual life of the thirties). Even with this concentration upon the more basic features we have had to skip that detailed examination which alone gives body and life to the reconstruction of the past.

My vast number of co-workers in the thirties would not thank me for recalling how they contributed to the era of "revisionism," for from 1945 onward they joined in its repudiation or kept silent—with few honorable exceptions. Indeed, in the whole spectrum of international Communist leadership, there was only a single voice raised in 1945 with a kind word in parting for an intimate associate of a quarter of a century's standing and that was Mao Tse-tung. And that was quickly erased by the censors, so that I learned of it only from the archivists when they dug it out twenty years later.

It is this contempt for history which is the sharpest feature that marks both the Russian and Chinese Communist leaders from Marx, the founder of their ideology. Marx, however stubbornly he clung to certain dogmas which were contradicted by facts, never denied the facts themselves. On the contrary, he meticulously recorded the facts, and looked for confirmation of his beloved dogma in the future development of history.